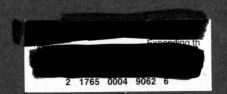

Expanding th

2 1765 0004 9062 6

D1071735

EXPANDING THE INTERNATIONAL DIMENSION OF HIGHER EDUCATION

Jossey-Bass Publishers
San Francisco • Washington • London • 1980

EXPANDING THE INTERNATIONAL DIMENSION OF HIGHER EDUCATION
Barbara B. Burn

Copyright © 1980 by: The Carnegie Foundation
for the Advancement of Teaching

Jossey-Bass Inc., Publishers
433 California Street
San Francisco, California 94104

Jossey-Bass Limited
28 Banner Street
London EC1Y 8QE

Copyright under International, Pan American, and Universal
Copyright Convention. All rights reserved. No part of this
book may be reproduced in any form—except for brief quotation
(not to exceed 1,000 words) in a review or professional
work—without permission in writing from The Carnegie Foundation
for the Advancement of Teaching and the publishers.

The Carnegie Council on Policy Studies in Higher Education,
2150 Shattuck Avenue, Berkeley, California 94704, has sponsored
publication of this report as part of a continuing effort to
obtain and present information for public discussion.
The views expressed are those of the author.

Copies are available from Jossey-Bass, San Francisco,
for the United States and Possessions, and for Canada,
Australia, New Zealand, and Japan.
Copies for the rest of the world are available from
Jossey-Bass, London.

Library of Congress Cataloging in Publication Data

Burn, Barbara B
    Expanding the international dimension of higher educa-
tion

    Bibliography: p. 157
    Includes index.
    1. Education, Higher—1965- 2. Universities and
colleges. 3. International education. 4. Research.
I. Title.
LB2322.B84   378   79-24879
ISBN 0-87589-444-5

Manufactured in the United States of America

JACKET DESIGN BY WILLI BAUM

FIRST EDITION

Code 8004

The Carnegie Council Series

The following publications are available from Jossey-Bass Inc., Publishers, 433 California Street, San Francisco, California 94104.

The Federal Role in Postsecondary
Education: Unfinished Business,
1975-1980
*The Carnegie Council on Policy
Studies in Higher Education*

More Than Survival: Prospects for
Higher Education in a Period
of Uncertainty
*The Carnegie Foundation for the
Advancement of Teaching*

Making Affirmative Action Work
in Higher Education: An Analysis
of Institutional and Federal
Policies with Recommendations
*The Carnegie Council on Policy
Studies in Higher Education*

Presidents Confront Reality: From
Edifice Complex to University
Without Walls
*Lyman A. Glenny, John R. Shea,
Janet H. Ruyle, Kathryn H. Freschi*

Progress and Problems in Medical
and Dental Education: Federal
Support Versus Federal Control
*The Carnegie Council on Policy
Studies in Higher Education*

Low or No Tuition: The Feasibility
of a National Policy for the
First Two Years of College
*The Carnegie Council on Policy
Studies in Higher Education*

Managing Multicampus Systems:
Effective Administration in an
Unsteady State
Eugene C. Lee, Frank M. Bowen

Challenges Past, Challenges
Present: An Analysis of
American Higher Education
Since 1930
David D. Henry

The States and Higher Education:
A Proud Past and a Vital Future
*The Carnegie Foundation for the
Advancement of Teaching*

Educational Leaves for Employees:
European Experience
for American Consideration
*Konrad von Moltke,
Norbert Schneevoigt*

Faculty Bargaining in Public
Higher Education: A Report and
Two Essays
*The Carnegie Council on Policy
Studies in Higher Education,
Joseph W. Garbarino, David E.
Feller, Matthew W. Finkin*

Selective Admissions in Higher
Education: Comment and
Recommendations and Two Reports
*The Carnegie Council on Policy
Studies in Higher Education,
Winton H. Manning, Warren W.
Willingham, Hunter M. Breland,
and Associates*

Investment in Learning: The
Individual and Social Value of
American Higher Education
*Howard R. Bowen
with the collaboration of Peter
Clecak, Jacqueline Powers Doud,
Gordon K. Douglass*

Curriculum: A History of
the American Undergraduate
Course of Study Since 1636
Frederick Rudolph

Missions of the College Curriculum:
A Contemporary Review with Sug-
gestions
*The Carnegie Foundation for the
Advancement of Teaching*

The States and Private
Higher Education: Problems
and Policies in a New Era
*The Carnegie Council on Policy
Studies in Higher Education*

Handbook on Undergraduate
Curriculum
Arthur Levine

Fair Practices in Higher Education:
Rights and Responsibilities of
Students and Their Colleges in a
Period of Intensified Competition
for Enrollments
*The Carnegie Council on Policy
Studies in Higher Education*

Next Steps for the 1980s
in Student Financial Aid:
A Fourth Alternative
*The Carnegie Council on Policy
Studies in Higher Education*

Giving Youth a Better Chance:
Options for Education, Work, and
Service
*The Carnegie Council on Policy
Studies in Higher Education*

*The following technical reports are available from the Carnegie
Council on Policy Studies in Higher Education, 2150 Shattuck Avenue,
Berkeley, California 94704.*

The States and Higher Education:
A Proud Past and a Vital Future
SUPPLEMENT to a Commentary of
The Carnegie Foundation for the
Advancement of Teaching
*The Carnegie Foundation for the
Advancement of Teaching*

Changing Practices in
Undergraduate Education
*Robert Blackburn, Ellen
Armstrong, Clifton Conrad,
James Didham, Thomas McKune*

Contents

Preface

This study was greatly aided by a Carnegie Council task force, chaired by James A. Perkins, which met in February 1978 to consider major issues to be addressed. The task force members were Steven K. Bailey, Carl Kaysen, Margaret MacVicar, John W. Nason, Francis X. Sutton, and Paul Ylvisaker. Also helpful in the preparation of the study was a seminar on "The International Dimensions of Higher Education," also chaired by James Perkins, held at the Aspen Institute for Humanistic Studies July 17-28, 1978. The members of this seminar represented government, foundations, higher education, research establishments, and professional associations involved with higher education, as well as several different countries: Iran, Italy, Japan, Kuwait, Mexico, Sweden, the United Kingdom, and the United States.

Apart from these two formal bodies, many individuals and organizations, too numerous to mention by name, contributed information and advice. Special mention should be made of various organizations whose staff members were particularly helpful or whose ongoing activities and concerns contributed to my understanding of international education. Among the former are the Division of International Education of the Office of Education, the Department of State, the Arms Control and Disarmament Agency, the Board for International Food and Agricultural Development of the Agency for International Development, and the International Education Project of the American Council on Education. The second group of organizations includes the Institute of International Education, for which I directed a study of American students in Western Europe; the National Association for Foreign Student Affairs; the International Programs and Studies Office and the International Affairs Committee of the National Association of State Universities and Land-Grant Colleges; the American Academy of Arts and Sciences, which included me in its June 22-23, 1978, conference on Overseas Advanced Research Centers; the Association of Departments of Foreign Languages of the Modern Language Association; and the Council on International Educational Exchange, for whom I chaired a task force for government liaison on study abroad.

Before completing this study, I became Executive Director of the President's Commission on Foreign Language and International Studies, appointed by President Carter on September 15, 1978, of which James A. Perkins is chairman. The existence of this commission augurs well for international education in the United States. However, in light of my involvement with the commission, it would be inappropriate for me to make detailed recommendations in this study on matters with which the commission is concerned. Nevertheless, the research for this study has been helpful to me as a staff member of the commission and (I hope) provides a state-of-the-art review that will be useful to the commission as it proceeds to fulfill its mandate.

Finally, the reader should note that the principal author of Chapter 6, "International Faculty Exchanges," is S. Frederick Starr.

Washington, D.C.   Barbara B. Burn
October 1979

The Author

Barbara B. Burn is director of international programs, University of Massachusetts, Amherst. She recently chaired a task force for government liaison on study abroad for the Council on International Educational Exchange. In 1978 she was appointed executive director of the President's Commission on Foreign Language and International Studies.

Introduction

Global Education Concerns of Higher Education for the 1980s and Beyond

Clark Kerr

Chairman
Carnegie Council on Policy Studies in Higher Education

It is hard to understand why Americans seem to know or care so little about the international dimensions of their lives, when it is so obvious that we share our world with men and women of different countries and cultures. Young people are likely to

Note: These introductory remarks reflect some of the observations and concerns of members of the Carnegie Council on Policy Studies in Higher Education that emerged during our several discussions on the subject matter of the chapters that follow.

Two major studies of the international dimensions of higher education were made under the sponsorship of the Carnegie Commission on Higher Education. The first, by Barbara B. Burn, with chapters by Clark Kerr, Philip Altbach, and James A. Perkins, was *Higher Education in Nine Countries* (1971). The second, by Irwin T. Sanders and Jennifer C. Ward, was *Bridges to Understanding* (1970). This study reviewed the development and status of international programs of American colleges and universities at the beginning of the 1970s. Another source of international perspectives in the work of the Carnegie Commission was provided by a series of essays about American higher education written from the point of view of authorities in different countries—Sir Eric Ashby of Great Britain (1971); Joseph Ben-David of Israel (1972); Michio Nagai of Japan (1975); and Alain Touraine of France (1974).

know more about prospects for life on other planets than they do about the problems of human survival faced by people in the less developed countries on earth. Many of them also have deep concerns for the quality of the environment in our own cities, rural areas, and wildernesses yet fail to comprehend that environmental problems are universal and that some of them ultimately require international solutions. Increasing numbers of students use their educational opportunities to prepare for careers in the professions, business, and industry, seemingly unaware that international competition and interdependence are now part of the reality for most modern business enterprises. Millions of Americans now travel to other countries during their lifetimes, but many of them either take care that the conditions of their visits replicate the comforts of home or seek out the curiosities and "wonders" of the places they go without relating them to international or intercultural themes.

Public concern for international affairs has never been widespread in the United States. For much of our history, we considered ourselves geographically isolated and were impatient with events beyond our borders that threatened to distract us from developing our own growing nation. These attitudes changed during World War II, when an understanding of other nations, including both our allies and our enemies, became essential to our defense. When the war ended, Americans were called upon to assist in the rebuilding of war-damaged countries in both hemispheres and in helping less developed countries improve their economies and technical capabilities. Although many of the experts we then had in the languages, cultures, and affairs of other nations during these periods did know more languages than most college graduates are likely to know now, some of them still lacked the knowledge and skills they needed to carry out their assignments effectively.

As our awareness of other parts of the world grew, the federal government stimulated international studies at colleges and universities by creating modest programs of support. But these efforts did not grow and, to a considerable extent, have since languished. National preoccupations with dissent and disruption on the nation's campuses and with civil rights and other domestic issues generally overshadowed international concerns in the minds of most Americans. Even the controversy and confusion surrounding our involvement in the war in Vietnam had strong domestic overtones related to the fairness of the draft and certain civil rights issues. Moreover, the success of the reconstruction of countries that were damaged by World War II and the increasing independence of less developed countries have appeared to reduce the need for American resources and expertise abroad. Finally; the disenchantment of many Americans with the peace-keeping effectiveness of international organizations has been translated into a new isolationism.

One question confronting American higher education and the American people at the beginning of the 1980s is whether the opportunities for expanding and improving international education that were lost in the 1960s should now be recovered. In the judgment of many, including the Carnegie Council on Policy Studies in Higher Education, the answer is yes, for several reasons:

- The proper concern of education is the whole world, not just a part of it. Any educational effort that, in its totality, concerns itself with less than what can be known about all countries and all peoples of the world is incomplete.
- Knowledge respects no national boundaries. What is proved to be certain by universal standards of scientific inquiry and evaluation is no less true in China or Brazil than it is in Russia or Canada or the United States. Intellectuals of all nations contribute to the scope of human knowledge and understanding.
- The ability of educated people to use what they know in the advancement of any human enterprise is greatly enlarged by the acquisition of knowledge and skills that enable them to function effectively in more than one country or culture.
- One of the central problems of all nations has become the use of nonrenewable resources. As Cleveland (1979, p. 130) said, "People who deplete their depletable resources too fast will sooner than necessary be leaning on others for those resources or substitutes for them. People who erode their own

soil, destroy their own wildlife, overcut their own forests, overfish their own coastal waters, may similarly be heading for the international dole. The peoples of other nations, especially those who will likely have to pick up the check, have asserted and will increasingly assert a right to be heard in international discourse, on these 'domestic' delinquencies."

• In many other matters—including the prevention of nuclear war and the arrest of inflation—international cooperation becomes increasingly crucial. Such cooperation cannot be effective unless substantial numbers of men and women in all countries have a good understanding of the people and conditions in other parts of the world. It is no longer good enough to know that countries and people are different. We now need to know how they are different, why they are different, and how the differences will affect cooperative efforts to achieve desired objectives.

• As Harlan Cleveland points out (1979, p. 133), international policy is increasingly determined by domestic policies because "national governments are not themselves very good at working in, or on, the domestic affairs of other nations." International relations have never, in the history of nations, been the business solely of kings, prime ministers, presidents, or their designated emissaries. They are also shaped and maintained by businessmen, missionaries, technical advisers and consultants, and tourists. Therefore, nations in which the global perspectives of large parts of the populations are well developed have an international advantage. More of their people are likely to understand the international implications of events and policies at home, and more of their people who have occasion to visit or conduct business abroad will have the capacity to make themselves and their country understood by others. Foreign policies negotiated among international leaders may, as a result, rest more solidly on a foundation of relationships among citizens.

• It is inconceivable that any country that aspires to international leadership can exercise that role if its people are undereducated in international affairs. Barbara Burn reports on a survey that rates 14-year-olds in the United States near the top among students in eight countries in their knowledge of local, state, and national affairs but "next to last" in their knowledge of world affairs.

It is now essential that the United States reverse the erosive trends in international education that have been with us for the past decade. More specifically, we need to:

1. Give more attention to global perspectives and languages in the development of the curriculum.
2. Continue to encourage students in other countries to study in the United States. Their presence in our classrooms contributes to world stability, peace, and mutual understanding.
3. Take steps to prevent exploitation of foreign students by institutions that seek only to bolster their own enrollments.
4. Take steps also to prevent foreign student exploitation of educational opportunities in the United States as a means simply of gaining entry to the country.
5. Devise better federal government mechanisms for the improvement and encouragement of ·international education. Although international education is not the responsibility solely of the federal government, there is a great need for federal leadership and effective national programs.
6. Develop the experts and library resources needed for international-education programs without concern for enrollment levels of such programs.
7. Recognize the importance of international scholarship not only for serving the national interest but also as a means of meeting long-term needs for intellectual competence in understanding various cultures in the world around us.

Global Perspectives in the Curriculum

Virtually all subjects in the social sciences and humanities are susceptible to interpretation from the perspectives of different cultures. Only mathematics and some of the physical sciences are comparatively constant throughout the world. Discussion of global perspectives in the curriculum very quickly, therefore, can become preoccupied with such questions as: Which perspectives should be presented? In which subjects is the international perspective most important? What resources are available for introducing the perspectives that are desired? Barbara Burn raises another difficult question—whether the selection of perspectives to be introduced reflects an American view of the world, thus reinforcing parochialism, or whether it reflects a genuine desire to see how other national or cultural perspectives interact with the subjects under study, thus broadening understanding.

As a practical matter, these questions will be answered in terms of a college's instructional resources and the character of the subject that is taught. However, there are opportunities in the teaching of many subjects at least to introduce comparative examples and evidence drawn from several cultures or countries. In some subjects, important principles and concepts have origins in several countries, and instructors should be able to identify not only the source of these ideas but also the conditions in the country or region of origin that help explain the ideas' emergence, definition, and influence.

The less subtle forms of international education involve courses and programs in international relations and area studies. Barbara Burns reports that about seven percent of all undergraduates were enrolled in such courses in 1970; fewer may be enrolled in such courses now because of reductions in federal support for area-studies centers.

One implication of the growing interdependence of nations is that people who are prepared not only for certain professions and occupations but also in the language and culture of another part of the world become especially valuable, particularly in business, as transnational economics and multinational corporations play larger roles in the decisions that have to be made by American firms. Some indicators of this growing internationalization of American interests are found in the following facts. Between 1960 and 1977, the value of U.S. imports of goods and services increased from $23.7 billion to $193.7 billion. Between 1960 and 1976, the value of our exports increased from $28.9 billion to $182.2 billion (*1979 World Almanac*); foreign investments in the United States increased from $8.8 billion to $30.2

billion; and American investments abroad increased from $31.9 billion to $137.2 billion (U.S. Bureau of Census, *Statistical Abstracts*). Evidence of expanded interest in the rest of the world by individual private American citizens can be found in the following:

- The number of American visitors abroad increased from 11.1 million in 1960 to 22.3 million in 1976.
- U.S. foreign travel expenditures increased from $2.3 billion to $9.4 billion in the same period.
- The number of American passports issued and renewed between 1960 and 1977 increased from 853,087 to 3,107,122.
- The number of foreign students enrolled in institutions of higher education in the United States increased from 53,100 in 1960-61 to 250,000 in 1978-79.
- The number of Americans studying abroad increased from 12,500 in 1962 to 70,000 in 1975.
- The number of U.S. college faculty members abroad increased from 3,793 in 1962 to 6,522 in 1975.

Particularly dramatic evidence of private interests in international matters is provided by the growth of multinational corporations, whose combined products now exceed the GNPs of most countries in the world. Solomon (1978) says that the sales of the foreign subsidiaries of multinational corporations totaled $450 billion in 1973, approximately one-half of which was generated by American firms. In the same year, the gross product (GP) of these corporations was exceeded only by the gross national product (GNP) of the United States ($1,289.1 billion) and exceeded, for example, that of Japan ($412.0 billion), West Germany ($319.7 billion), France ($247.6 billion), and the United Kingdom ($171.1 billion) (U.S. Bureau of the Census, 1974, p. 824).

The efforts made in behalf of international education in colleges and universities contrast sharply with the growth of international interests of the government, business and private individuals. For example:

- In 1960, 17 percent of American college and university students were enrolled in foreign-language classes; by 1977 this had decreased to 8 percent.
- In 1966, 89 percent of U.S. colleges and universities required a foreign language; by 1974 this had decreased to 53 percent.
- NDEA Title VI area centers decreased from 107 in 1970 to 80 in 1978.
- Appropriations for NDEA Title VI programs went from $13 million in 1970 to $17 million in 1978—but were still significantly less than the $75 million authorized.
- NDEA fellowships decreased from 2,400 in 1969-70 to 835 in 1974-75.
- Federal funding of foreign-affairs-related contract and grant research decreased from $40.6 million in 1967-68 to $32.6 million in 1976-77.
- In the mid-1960s, 800-900 American students per year received postgraduate awards from the Institute of International Education (Fulbrights and others); by the mid-1970s, only 350 such fellowships per year were awarded.

As a first step away from a fractional view of humanity, colleges and universities should make provision for students who want to combine studies in an academic or occupational specialty with a foreign language and studies of some other part of the world. In fact, there is something to be said for the argument that all Americans need to be bilingual and that colleges and high schools share the responsibility for achieving that goal. One way that some colleges have worked toward that objective in the past has been to require that all entering students have one year of foreign language study in high school on their record. They have enforced that standard by awarding credit for the first year of any language instruction in college only when it involves instruction in a student's second foreign language. Despite such practices, foreign-language instruction has declined in popularity and importance in both schools and colleges. In the 1960s, foreign languages were victims of the policies of colleges and universities that reduced graduation requirements generally in response to student preference for more electives.

Language instruction is now in trouble as an early victim of the adjustment colleges are making to declining enrollments and limited financial resources.

Among the reasons frequently cited for the decline in foreign-language instruction is the fact that English is now the leading world language and Americans therefore expect to be able to speak and be understood in their own tongue wherever they go. This argument overlooks the fact that students of a foreign language acquire more than communication skills. They also acquire insights into the cultures of other countries and broaden their own perspectives of the things, attitudes, and occurrences they find in their daily lives by seeing how they are viewed from perspectives of a culture and tradition different from their own. One suggestion we have for colleges and universities is that they make these values more explicit. Students should be taught about foreign cultures and institutions at the same time they learn the languages themselves. To facilitate and improve such instruction, teachers of foreign languages in the United States might be asked to receive part of their training at colleges in other countries.

Another reason cited for the decline of the teaching of languages in American schools and colleges is that European cultures now have less influence on the United States than they did in earlier times. In our judgment, this is an unfortunate miscalculation of the true interdependence of our country and other countries, not just in Europe but elsewhere.

An additional reason cited for decline of foreign-language instruction is that languages have been poorly taught in high schools. It is alleged that such instruction has not instilled in students either a love for languages or a desire for further studies of foreign languages or cultures.

One consequence of decreasing enrollments in foreign languages is that students who plan to teach these subjects may become discouraged by poor job prospects; this could adversely affect teacher quality for many years to come. Another consequence is that American college graduates who enter increasingly internationalized occupations and professions may find themselves disadvantaged because of their inadequate language skills. Similar handicaps will be felt by the men and women who take advantage of increasing opportunities to travel abroad; because they will be ill prepared in the languages, customs, and cultures of the countries they visit.

Many colleges and universities provide opportunities for their students to spend a semester or a year abroad in studies that yield credit toward a degree. In some instances, special arrangements are made with existing colleges and universities in other countries for this purpose; in a few cases, colleges create branches abroad; in other instances, students are encouraged to make independent arrangements and study under the same conditions that are experienced by native students in the countries they live. Unknown numbers of American students simply stop out of college or delay attendance after graduating from high school in order to spend some time on independent travel.

Colleges and universities with formal study-abroad programs obviously have a responsibility to make sure that the students who participate in them are properly prepared, not only in the language but also in aspects of the general culture and the level of academic instruction to be encountered in the countries they visit. Most students should be carefully and thoroughly counseled before they leave the United States so that they know what to expect and will understand their limitations and opportunities as learners in another land. Consideration should also be given to greater use of students who have spent time in other countries as resources for instruction after they return. They might, for example, serve as language tutors or participate in "debriefing" programs in classes where their experiences are relevant or in sessions open to all interested persons in the campus community.

An increased familiarity with the people and cultures of other countries is becoming a valuable asset of any well-educated person. For these reasons, international components should be included in the general education programs of both secondary schools and colleges. Language instruction should begin in American schools as early as educationally possible, and evaluations of competence should be substituted for the amount of time spent in a foreign-language class as a means of determining a student's readiness to advance to higher levels. Both parents and employers need to be more aware than many of them now seem to be of the advantages of foreign-language skills and interests in other countries for the nation's youth. Such skills and knowledge make one a more useful employee and a more effective citizen of the world.

Foreign Students as a Learning Resource

Formal courses and programs in international studies and foreign languages are not the only sources of learning with global perspectives. Students also learn from each other, and the 250,000 students from other countries who are now studying in American colleges and universities are an underutilized resource for improved communication between cultures.

It is important to future relations between the United States and other countries that foreign students come to understand us—to learn what goals are important to Americans and what we expect from our relationship with other countries. It is reasonable to expect that, because many of the foreign students in the United States come from the ablest sectors of their own societies, they will return to positions of leadership and influence at home after their education is completed. It is hoped that they can also be accurate interpreters of our country's policies to their own people.

While they are here, foreign students should be given ample opportunities to participate fully in the life of our college and university campuses and in the communities that surround them. They may need, and should be given, special assistance in maneuvering through the regulations and procedures encountered on campus, in acquiring competence in the English language (to the extent they may have deficiencies), and in other matters. Every effort should be made to determine as precisely as possible what they expect from their American educational experiences and, to the extent that it is appropriate and feasible, to help them to get it. Such assistance is nothing more than part of our colleges' responsibilities as hosts to foreign visitors.

Inasmuch as foreign students constitute only about two percent of the enrollment of American colleges and universities, it is doubtful that the special attention that should be extended to them will be burdensome. Moreover, it can be repaid many times over by imaginatively utilizing their natural expertise in their own cultures to enrich the international perspectives of American students on the host campuses. They may be used to assist in language instruction, in contributing to seminars on societal characteristics of their homelands, as tutors in esoteric languages, and in many other ways. Part of the responsibility of foreign-student advisers on college campuses should be to develop, with the cooperation of members of the faculty, programs that effectively utilize the instructional resources foreign students can provide. The federal government should provide funding for activities that utilize foreign students constructively in undergraduate education. This could be done as part of the NDEA Title VI support for innovative undergraduate programs in international studies and through support provided by the National Endowment for the Arts and the National Endowment for the Humanities for programs relating to the arts and contributions to humanistic learning of other countries. Individual institutions should also provide for such programs.

If colleges and universities are to get the greatest possible educational benefit from the learning opportunities afforded by their foreign students, they should keep in mind that students do not come from all parts of the globe in equal numbers; furthermore, they may not represent the full diversity of international cultures. For example, nearly one-fifth of all foreign students in the United States now come from OPEC nations. Foreign students also may be overconcentrated in certain academic disciplines—engineering, for example, or business and management. Where it is possible for them to do so, colleges should try to diversify the foreign representation on their campuses.

The most important principle that institutions should observe in admitting foreign students, however, is that all students (native or foreign) should be admitted only after it is determined that they are likely to accomplish their academic goals. Although we strongly favor college and university efforts to attract students broadly representative of other countries to their campuses, we do feel a warning is in order. Some colleges may welcome foreign students for the wrong reasons—just to fill their classrooms and dormitories, for example. In fact, in some countries, educational brokers capitalize on this situation by recruiting young men and women in wholesale numbers for American colleges and universities. Not all foreign student intermediaries are unscrupulous; many are legitimate, providing their services at fair prices, representing the educational opportunities they offer accurately, and making certain that the students they recruit are qualified for completing their education at an American institution successfully. Some agencies, however, lead their clients to believe that all American colleges and universities are of the same quality or that a degree will be equally valuable whether it is earned at a prestigious institution or not. They also minimize the importance of knowing how to speak English or cope with other basic learning skills before entering colleges. Some of their clients may arrive on an American campus that is not prepared to give them the special services they need to move smoothly into a new academic and societal life. The blame for such misrepresentation and exploitation of foreign students cannot be placed entirely on recruiters and brokers, however. Much of it falls on the shoulders of colleges and universities that accept students and services from these individuals and agencies without adequate prior investigation. Unscrupulous operators could not exist if American institutions refused to admit their clients or condone their practices.

Even when foreign students arrange for admission to an American institution on their own, or through the auspices of reputable foreign agencies, the host institutions have some basic responsibilities:

- They should make certain that they have accurately represented themselves to the students who come to them. This includes making certain that the students understand differences between American colleges and universities and those of their homelands.

- They should administer admissions requirements in such a way that no dispensations granted to foreign students will impair their opportunities for academic success.
- They should provide services and staff to assist foreign students in their adjustment to the campus.
- They also may need to provide tutoring to overcome some students' deficiencies in subject mastery and learning skills that were overlooked in the admissions process.

The integrity of the American higher-education programs offered to foreign students also should be protected from abuse by young people who might want to exploit them. Opportunities for youth are not equal in all societies of the world. Political and social conditions in some countries may lead young people to seek out circumstances that are more comfortable than those at home. One place they may look is the United States, which they enter by being admitted to American colleges. Some foreign students have been known to pay their tuitions and disappear once they have enrolled. Americans were surprised to learn, after seeing a television film of Iranian "students" demonstrating in front of the shah's mother's house in southern California, that the U.S. Immigration Service was unable to provide accurate information about the actual number of Iranian students in this country. In fact, none of the currently available foreign-student enrollment figures is totally reliable. Both higher-education institutions and the appropriate government agencies need to cooperate in systematically reporting and verifying the current academic status of students from other countries.

The Challenge to Colleges and Universities

Much of what Barbara Burn writes about in this book concerns national policies and programs. Readers should not conclude from her discussions, however, that all of the challenges and opportunities associated with expanding the international dimension of higher education must be met with national solutions. As we shall note presently, the federal government has important roles to play, but much can be done by institutions acting independently.

Erosion of foreign-language instruction in the United States has been the result, for the most part, of institutional decisions that placed student demands ahead of intellectual and national interests. This trend can be reversed whenever colleges and universities choose to give foreign languages a higher place in their own educational priorities. Similarly, any initiative that involves enlarging international perspectives in the curriculum can be taken by departments, schools, and colleges within institutions of higher education. Moving in that direction requires, above all, that encouragement come not only in the form of explicit institution-wide statements of educational policy but also of incentives and rewards for faculty members and departments that consciously advance that policy. Much of the administrative and coordinating machinery needed in internationalizing higher education already exists on many campuses, but additional efforts may be required in the counseling of foreign students and American students planning to study abroad, in evaluating applications of foreign students for admission, and in providing special instructional assistance to foreign students as needed.

Beyond the measures that can be taken on the campuses, the leaders of American colleges and universities have a responsibility and opportunity to exert leadership in the cause of expanding the international dimension of learning at all levels of the nation's educational system. Such leadership is needed within colleges and universities to generate and sustain an interest in the international context among faculties and the various internal divisions of instruction and research. It is needed off campus to persuade secondary schools to participate in the effort; to persuade parents of college students that the internationalization of higher learning increases the value of a college education to the individual; and to persuade prospective employers of college graduates that they, too, can benefit from national efforts to increase the global awareness and language skills of the men and women who will be working for them in the future.

After all, the case for internationalization of American education is not difficult to make. Increasingly, the economic and political interests of our country are affected by circumstances and events abroad. The current energy crisis is perhaps the most dramatic (although not the only) example. Inflation, unemployment, technological advancement, and, of course, national security are all influenced by global conditions. Our nation's ability to build friendly and peaceful relationships with other countries depends to a considerable extent upon its ability to contribute to the stability and progress of the peoples of many lands.

The Role of the Federal Government

Since national, as well as private, interests are potentially so well served by the cultivation of international perspectives among our people, it is surprising that the federal government has thus far made only tentative efforts to support international education.

The most significant efforts by the federal government today are the provisions of the National Defense Education Act of 1958 (NDEA) and its subsequent amendments. The act originally was passed when there was general concern for national preparedness and scientific and technological competition with Russia. Title VI of the legislation provides support for language and area-study centers within educational institutions and consortia. It also provides funding for the development of instructional resources in international studies, introduction of international perspectives into existing instruction, outreach activities aimed at schools and other institutions, and research in international studies.

The federal government also supports programs that enable students and scholars from other countries to study, teach, and engage in research in the United States. Through the Fulbright scholarship program, 80,000 foreign nationals and 41,000 Americans have been given such support since 1949. Barbara Burn notes that, although the number of foreign students supported by the program dropped from an average 1,800 annually during 1949-1968 to about half that number in the early 1970s, the number increased to more than 1,900 in 1978. Somewhat less support has been available for American faculty members studying abroad. Under the Fulbright program, only 10 percent of American scholars abroad were given federal assistance. In 1977-78, this included 530 lecturers and research scholars. The total U.S. contribution to the Fulbright exchange of scholars and students in 1978-79 was nearly $20 million, compared with over $28 million in 1966-67, the peak year. Burn points out that if, in the course of a 40-year career, every American faculty member were able to spend one semester abroad every 10 years, it would be necessary to increase the numbers going abroad every year fivefold. Although it is not clear that this is a realistic or desirable goal from the standpoint of improving international education in the United States, it at least suggests a considerable margin for improving the situation that exists. The General Accounting Office is now reviewing the exchange-of-persons programs of the federal government to determine how they can be made more effective. As Burn suggests, the Fulbright program might also be reviewed to determine how well the scholars involved are prepared for their overseas activities and to assess the contribution of the Fulbright program administered by the U.S. Office of Education, which sponsored almost 700 scholars abroad between 1964 and 1976.

During the 1950s and 1960s, the technical assistance of specialists from American colleges and universities frequently was called upon by less developed countries of the world. Initially, such effort emphasized the development of higher education and the national economies of the countries involved. Since 1973, the emphasis has shifted to assistance for countries with very low per-capita incomes. National legislation in 1975 sought to improve the capacities of United States land-grant and other eligible universities to participate in international efforts to "apply more effective agricultural sciences to the goal of increasing world food production, and in general . . . provide increased and longer term support to the application of science to solving food and nutrition problems of the developing countries." Such activities now account for about 55 percent of the budget of the Agency for International Development (AID), which was created in 1961.

The involvement of colleges and universities in AID programs is still not extensive, however. Only 68 universities held contracts for technical service in agriculture and rural development with the agency in 1976-77, and in fall 1975 only 5 percent of the institutions in the American Association of State Colleges and Universities had international development contracts with less developed countries. Several proposals for the reorganization of technical-assistance programs are now under consideration, however, and it is hoped that scientific and technological programs and research, both in the United States and in the less developed countries, will expand and that participation of our colleges and universities in such activities will become more effective as a result.

Federal interest in the global dimension of higher education appeared to be very strong in 1966, when Congress passed an international education act that stated:

> The Congress hereby finds and declares that a knowledge of other countries is of utmost importance in promoting mutual understanding and cooperation between nations; that strong American educational resources are a necessary base for strengthening our relations with other countries; that this and future generations of Americans should be assured ample opportunity to develop to the fullest extent possible their intellectual capacities in all areas of knowledge pertaining to other countries, peoples, and cultures; and that it is therefore both necessary and appropriate for the Federal Government to assist in the development of resources and trained personnel in academic and professional fields, and to coordinate the existing and future programs of the Federal Government in international education to meet the requirements of world leadership.

Congress authorized appropriations for provisions of this act that would reach $90 million for fiscal year 1969 alone, and colleges and universities all over the country created international offices and programs in anticipation of opportunities to participate in the activities it contemplated. But the act was never funded, and the seriousness of the federal government's interest in international studies is now regarded with skepticism on college campuses.

There are a few bright spots. For example, as Barbara Burn notes, Ernest Boyer, when U.S. Commissioner of Education, repeatedly asserted that global education was one of his priorities, and a task force was organized in his office to investigate the implications of that emphasis. Another encouraging sign has been the appointment of the Commission on Foreign Language and International Studies by President Carter in 1978, of which Burn has served as executive director. The newly organized International Communication Agency, which assumed responsibilities formerly exercised by the U.S. Information Agency and the State Department's Bureau of Education and Cultural Affairs, has an official mandate to increase the American people's knowledge and understanding of other countries. And the National Endowment for the Humanities has demonstrated increasing interest in providing support for international scholarship and education for global understanding.

We strongly believe that the federal government should make firm commitments to support programs that stimulate international scholarship, foreign-language studies, exchange of students and faculty members among nations, and cultivation of intellectual, technical, and creative resources on the nation's campuses that will facilitate American assistance and participation in cooperative efforts in other parts of the world. But the commitments must be more than an articulation of intentions. Once disappointed by strong assertions of federal interest in the international dimensions of higher education that proved to be unsupported by tangible programs and support, colleges and universities may well be reluctant to commit their own limited and, in some cases, dwindling resources to such efforts unless the federal government provides financial as well as moral support for such endeavors. One way for the federal government to demonstrate the seriousness of its concerns for international education would be to strengthen current programs and take advantage of opportunities that already exist. We encourage the federal government to:

- Provide for the use of funds for international education and for financial aid generally to support study abroad so that it is a genuine option for students who might otherwise be unable to afford it.
- Pursue the mandate of the International Communication Agency (ICA) to acquaint Americans with other cultures and peoples in ways that include college students among target groups.
- Maintain sufficient funding for NDEA Title VI centers to make possible the implementation of Section 603, which is intended to "stimulate locally designed educational programs to increase the understanding of students in the United States about the cultures and actions of other nations in order to better evaluate the international and domestic impact of major national policies."
- Double the level of funding for undergraduate international studies administered by the Office of Education and increase the time period for grants from the current two-year limit for individual institutions and three years for consortia to three years for individual institutions and four years for consortia.
- Continue federal funding of programs to increase the expertise of study-abroad administrators, mainly through ICA support of such programs organized by nongovernmental organizations. A major goal should be to strengthen study abroad as a priority activity of colleges and universities.
- Financially support a full revival of the Fulbright exchange program in a manner that will enable it to attract the best potential participants.
- Provide financial support on a long-term basis for other major exchanges, including those with the U.S.S.R., Eastern Europe, and the People's Republic of China.
- Increase the federal funding of Title VI area- and international-studies centers and programs from the $9.4 million provided in 1978-79 to $12 million in 1980-81, with increases at least to keep pace with inflation thereafter.
- Create a national center to collect, on a continuing basis, data on area specialists by country or region, language, and discipline. This would be a useful step toward monitoring and

maintaining the pool of competencies needed by government, higher education, business, and other sectors of society.
· Fund foreign-affairs research at the level of $10 to $15 million annually. A new federal agency should be established to administer these funds and, to be effective, should be as independent as possible, and should award grants on a peer-review basis.

Protecting Basic Resources

A fully mature effort to introduce and sustain international perspectives on a college or university campus requires the development of certain basic services and resources. Among them are adequate counseling and advising services for foreign students and for American students contemplating study abroad; experts on different countries and geographic regions; personnel to maintain liaison with government agencies, other institutions, and consortia and with associations and businesses that have international interests; and library resources to support strong international-study programs. It is unrealistic and undesirable for every institution to create all of these resources or to cover every possible country or area, much less every international issue, in depth. But every institution should have sufficient resources to reflect multinational interests and concerns in general. Beyond that, some colleges and universities should also attempt to develop depth in one or several country, area, or international-interest fields. Through cooperative arrangements with other institutions and consortia, colleges and universities should also make the faculty members and specialized library resources of neighboring institutions available to their own students.

In times like the present, when financial resources that are available are so frequently adequate only to the demands of immediate student interests, institutions may be tempted to allow enrollment trends alone, as an index of student interest, to determine the level of their efforts to cultivate the international perspective in their instruction and research programs. While such policies are practical in the narrow context of one institution at a moment in history, they betray a misunderstanding of long-range realities. Capabilities for infusing our educational efforts with international perspectives constitute a national resource of considerable consequence. The need for specialists and for specialized knowledge in the international field is not constantly the same. It is felt unevenly and shifts with the sometimes erratic flow of history. Anticipating such needs requires that the sources of training and study about other countries and international issues exist somewhere on a sustained basis and that they do not appear and disappear in response to enrollment demands alone.

Enlarging the Human Perspective

There is much more involved in international education than the national interest alone. Modern men and women need to be aware of their place and potential in the context of an international environment. This awareness is as essential as the continuing need for awareness of our place and progress in the context of history and of our limitations and possibilities in the context of the laws of basic science. The time long ago arrived for Americans to develop an awareness of international perspectives through the infusion of these perspectives into the curriculum and their systematic study by scholars. As we respond to the potentials of such development, the benefits will transcend the interests of both individuals and our nation. We shall also contribute to an expansion of the culture and thought and knowledge of men and women in these increasingly international times.

Higher education, among other important purposes, helps to prepare individuals and the nation for the future, and the future now holds more global and fewer strictly national dimensions. Higher education is also a central component of knowledge systems, and knowledge systems are now international; they even involve outer space. We need a new vision for higher education that goes beyond the land-grant, or even urban-grant, tradition—that orients its activities in the words of the Rockefeller Foundation's statement of purpose, to the "well-being of mankind throughout the world." The great problem of the world is the future of the world, including the depletion of the resources of nature and the instability of the world political order. Higher education in its more constuctive periods had always been oriented toward the understanding of the life, the tensions, the problems, and the solutions of the times.

The universities of the Middle Ages were part of the Western civilization of their day. In the intervening centuries, universities have become more nationalized, more devoted to national concerns: The building of a better civil service in France, the modernization of agriculture and industry in the United States, the building of a communist state in Russia, the creation of an indigenous leadership elite in many formerly colonial societies are examples. Now, a new stage may be evolving in which the university once again becomes part of world civilization rather than the servant of one political entity alone. A new role for higher education may be emerging: the cultivation of thought about the future of world society.

Students raised on nightly TV news programs are ready. Colleges are also ready to use their resources, particularly as they face decreased demand in some traditional areas of study. But they need some encouragement and financial assistance from the federal government. The nation is more and more involved in world political and economic leadership. Yet higher education has been in retreat in its attention to the international dimensions of the world for the past two decades (Figure 1).[1] This trend needs to be reversed. The nation and the world are moving in exactly opposite directions from higher education. Higher education has not been leading. It has not been following. It has been going the wrong way.

[1]Note, in particular, in Figure 1 the declines in activities classified under "international decisions affecting higher education," while almost all other listed activities have increased. Higher education, apparently, has been moving in one direction, and individuals, economic enterprises, and general federal policy in another. Higher education has become more parochial, in some of its endeavors, as the rest of American society has, in important dimensions, become more cosmopolitan.

Figure 1. Trends in selected decisions in international contexts

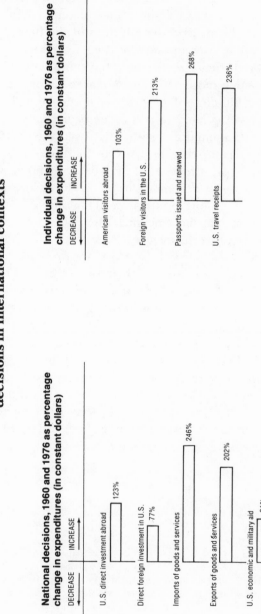

National decisions, 1960 and 1976 as percentage change in expenditures (in constant dollars)

DECREASE | INCREASE

U.S. direct investment abroad — 123%
Direct foreign investment in U.S. — 77%
Imports of goods and services — 246%
Exports of goods and services — 202%
U.S. economic and military aid — 91%

Individual decisions, 1960 and 1976 as percentage change in expenditures (in constant dollars)

DECREASE | INCREASE

American visitors abroad — 103%
Foreign visitors in the U.S. — 213%
Passports issued and renewed — 268%
U.S. travel receipts — 236%

(continued on next page)

Figure 1 (continued)

Institutional decisions affecting higher education as percentage change, selected periods

DECREASE | INCREASE

Colleges and universities requiring
foreign languages, 1967 and 1974
20%

NDEA Title VI area centers,
1972 and 1978
25%

Appropriations for NDEA
Title VI, 1970 and 1978
22%

NDEA fellowships,
1969–70 and 1974–75
65%

Persons involved in direct American/foreign
teacher exchanges, 1960 and 1978
17%

Peace Corps volunteers teaching secondary
level English abroad, 1967 and 1977
82%

Ford Foundation commitment of funds for
international education, 1966 and 1978
95%

Note: Some, but not all, of the time periods used in this figure do not correspond with those used in the text.

Sources: *National decisions (non-higher education):* U.S. Bureau of the Census, *Statistical Abstracts,* appropriate years.

Individual decisions (non-higher education): American and foreign

Individual decisions affecting higher education as percentage change, selected periods

DECREASE | INCREASE

Foreign students in U.S. colleges
and universities, 1961 and 1978
343%

American students studying abroad,
1962 and 1975
460%

U.S. college faculty abroad,
1963 and 1973
72%

Students enrolled in modern foreign language courses,
U.S. colleges and universities, 1960 and 1977
53%

visitors, travel receipts: U.S. Department of Commerce (n.d.). Passports: *1979 World Almanac.*

Institutional decisions (higher education): Languages: Caroux, 1977. Teacher exchanges: Compiled from information from U.S. Department of Health, Education, and Welfare, Office of Education, Teacher Exchange Section. Peace Corps: Allen (1978). Ford Foundation: Personal communication.

Individual decisions (higher education): Foreign students in U.S.: Julian and Slattery (1978). American students abroad: Institute of International Education (1977a), Perkins (1971), Academy for Educational Development (1975), and UNESCO (1975). Faculty abroad: National Center for Education Statistics, *Digest of Education Statistics,* appropriate years. Students in language courses: Modern Language Association (1978b).

EXPANDING THE INTERNATIONAL DIMENSION OF HIGHER EDUCATION

PREPARED FOR THE CARNEGIE COUNCIL
ON POLICY STUDIES IN HIGHER EDUCATION

1

International Education in Perspective

The purpose of this study is twofold: (1) to review the current status of international education in higher education in the United States and (2) to indicate current and future needs in this broad field. It is assumed, of course, that there are in fact significant needs in international education and that it must move in new directions if those needs are to be met. But,before discussing those new directions, it is necessary to be fully aware of the current state of the art.

In *An Owl Before Dusk,* Michio Nagai (1975, p. 39) remarked that the more important problems now are increasingly international, and only minor problems remain national. And in *A Passion for Paradox,* Harlan Cleveland (1977a, p. 7) observed that we now live "in a world where everything leads to everything else." As these statements imply, international education must reach more people and more professions. At the same time, it must preserve the best of existing international-studies training and research programs.

Since World War II, international education has tended to react to shifting currents in international relations. In the early postwar period, the Fulbright program was the intellectual counterpart to the Marshall Plan, launching an international

exchange of scholars that paralleled the massive economic cooperation undertaken by the United States and Europe. The cold
war brought with it a greater emphasis on the training of foreign-language and area-studies specialists. In the 1960s, the need
for greater understanding between nations stimulated increased
interest in international education. In that period, the primary
goal of international education was to help the foreign-aid program lead the developing nations toward prosperity and democracy, using America as a model. Central to the thinking of those
years was the need for "sensitive awareness of . . . cultural
pluralism" (Committee on the College and World Affairs
[CCWA], 1964, p. vii) and for knowledge about the growing
number of newly independent nations. With the Vietnam War
and its aftermath came a general disenchantment with international involvement, an apathy that was abruptly ended by the
energy crisis of 1973.

The most recent phase in international education reflects a
new awareness of the interdependence of nations. Issues that
were formerly regarded as domestic have become international.
Decisions and conditions in other parts of the world are blamed
for rising prices and fuel shortages in the United States. A new
thrust in international education is to instill a "global perspective" in all aspects of education. But persuasive as it may be, the
new jargon of interdependence, global perspective, and "space-
ship earth" threatens to obscure urgent aims and needs of international education.

Global perspective can mean simply that all issues and disciplines have an international context. However, it can also
imply that education should aspire to a "whole-world" outlook.
This may cause some people to forget that the perspectives of
other nations may be considerably less "global" than that of the
United States. This fact—with its deep roots in values, traditions, and situations that differ profoundly from our own—
should be kept in mind when considering trends in international
education. Otherwise the notion of a global perspective could
serve to legitimate a new brand of American parochialism.

The word *interdependence* can also be misleading. Its use
can mask the fact that U.S. dependence on other nations, while

it may have increased in some respects, is still minor compared with the dependence of other nations on the United States. This point is not lost on those nations, which feel their dependence much more than we feel ours and may view talk of interdependence as a smokescreen intended to disguise the true state of affairs. Americans should be aware of this situation and not be deceived that the United States is less potent than it really is. As one foreign observer has noted, most Americans do not realize how many of the decisions made in the rest of the world are determined by conditions in the United States.

Among the current and future needs in international education is a broader and deeper appreciation of foreign perspectives. Global and multinational problems exist in a world of cultural diversity that Americans are all too ready to discount as backwardness, to be remedied by scientific progress, technological and managerial aid, and ethical and political change. It may well be that in the next two decades Americans will be greatly surprised by the resilience of non-Western traditions—as has already been evidenced by the recent ouster of the shah of Iran. All of this argues against neglecting traditional approaches to international education in the rush to grapple with global problems and discover universal truths.[1]

Some Definitions

For the purposes of this study, *international education* is defined extremely broadly. In order to prepare Americans to live in an increasingly interrelated world, international education must involve "a major transformation of the entire educational system" (Lambert, 1978); where higher education is concerned, this implies that virtually the total curriculum must be transformed so that it can serve as a vehicle for increased knowledge about other countries and greater recognition of the transnational character of most issues.

One part of international education consists of interna-

---

[1]In this discussion of interdependence and global perspectives, I am indebted to E. Raymond Platig, Director of External Research in the Bureau of Intelligence and Research, Department of State.

tional studies. *International studies* has traditionally included mainly the study of foreign countries and regions—commonly referred to as *foreign-area studies* or *area studies*—and international relations. *International relations* focuses on the interactions and interrelationships among governments and other organizations, public and private, as well as individuals, and typically is taught in political science departments. Students majoring in international relations frequently aspire to careers in the foreign service or to other government employment involving relations with other countries. *Area studies,* in contrast, tend to be interdisciplinary, involving such fields as political science, history, literature, sociology, and the foreign language of the region or country concerned. Recent events in Iran suggest that theology can also be an important component of area studies. The student with a major in area studies usually gets a degree in a specific discipline rather than in area studies as such. To achieve significant specialization, the student must pursue postgraduate study as well as fieldwork, advanced study, or research in the foreign country or region. In the past, the great majority of area-studies specialists have found employment in the teaching profession, although a significant minority have entered government or business. Whereas international-relations students have usually studied the commonly taught Western European languages, area-studies specialists study the less commonly taught or non-Western languages, such as Arabic, Russian, and Chinese.

International studies, thus including international relations and area studies, is only one part of international education, however. International education also includes comparative, transnational, and so-called global studies, which focus more on issues and problems than on specific areas. Although international and global studies should be complementary, all too often they are viewed as competitive in terms of objectives, institutional priorities, and funding. Foreign-language study is regarded as a route to "global understanding" but is not essential to the concept of global studies.

International education addresses both approach and content. In terms of content, it assumes that a subject or discipline can no longer be understood if it focuses only on the U.S. experience. Almost no discipline is "culture free"; therefore, excluding the experience of other cultures from the teaching of a discipline that has a cultural context shortchanges the student and reflects an ill-advised chauvinism. (An example is history, which until recently was taught almost exclusively from an American point of view.) In terms of approach, international education calls for presenting a subject in an international framework so that students are aware of the interrelatedness of all nations and of the commonality of such problems as poverty and discrimination. In addition, students should be able to acknowledge the fact that other countries may be solving these problems more effectively than the United States.

By studying a subject in its international context, American students, especially those in professional fields, can acquire attitudes and knowledge that will enable them to see that most issues are international. They may then use this perspective in applying their professional training abroad as well as at home.

Higher education has already been "internationalized" to some extent. Social science and humanities departments offer courses dealing with other cultures and with international issues. Considerable progress has been made in this area. For example, a recent study shows that the percentage of doctorates in the social sciences and humanities focusing on the non-Western world or on topics of an international character awarded by 16 major research universities increased from 13 percent in 1940 to 20 percent in 1960 and 27 percent in 1976 (McCaughey, 1979).

For international education to be effective, however, not only should more courses be offered on other countries (especially non-Western countries) and on international topics but the entire curriculum should be permeated by an international outlook. This happens more readily at institutions whose faculty spend time teaching, doing research, and attending conferences outside the United States. This international outlook is more likely—but not assured—at research universities, which enroll close to 40 percent of the foreign students pursuing graduate study in the United States. It is also more likely—but again not assured—at institutions whose administrative staff is committed to this effort. And finally, it is more likely in professions whose members are becoming more interested in internationalization, such as business administration and law.

The attempt to transform American higher education in this way is an enormous undertaking, the progress of which cannot easily be measured. International courses in engineering, public health, or business administration will rarely include the word *international* in their titles. (The recent *Report to Congress on Arms Control Education and Academic Study Centers* was notable in identifying "course segments" in this field; U.S. Arms Control and Disarmament Agency [ACDA], 1979.) Hence, identifying all the courses currently offered that take an international perspective would be a formidable task, and as a result a careful assessment of the extent to which American higher education has become internationalized is, regrettably, well beyond the scope of this study.

Because of these limitations, this study deals primarily with international studies in the traditional sense while also discussing the opportunities for internationalization offered by foreign-language teaching, student and faculty exchanges, and development assistance projects involving institutions of higher education in less developed countries. To set the stage, recent changes in the international community and in American higher education are examined in the following sections.

The Changing International Community

Today, as in the past, international education is being shaped by changes in the international community and in the relative position of the United States within that community. Among these changes are the growing interdependence of all nations, both rich and poor; the emergence of new actors on the international stage; prospects for increased cross-cultural contact; and the continuing need for the United States to learn from other countries. I will discuss each of these developments in turn.

The Interdependence of Nations

Living as we do in a world where everything leads to everything else, conditions in the poor nations increasingly impinge on conditions in the rich ones. The endless litany of the world's problems, so familiar after the initial shock, has been vividly summarized by James Cameron (1978, p. 1): "There are 250 million children in the world who do not go to school. Last year the world spent more than 60 times more equipping each soldier than educating each child. Seventy percent of the human race lacks safe water. Waterborne disease kills 25,000 people a day. 570 million are officially undernourished. What the hell. These kind of figures have no meaning. However, we continue to spend on instruments of destruction a billion dollars a day." The point is not the existence of poverty, disease, hunger, and overcrowding; rather, the point is that the future of the United States and other advanced nations is threatened by these things. In the words of former AID administrator J. Gilligan (1978, pp. 2, 6), "With the single exception of the nuclear holocaust, all [major global] problems are concentrated in the third-world countries. If we're going to deal with them, we're going to deal with them in the third-world countries. . . . We're not running a global soup kitchen; we're attempting to deal with the very forces which will shape the world that our children are going to live in by the year 2000."

Too often, recitals of the enormous problems facing the less developed world are cast in terms of humanitarianism or morality. However, as Great Britain's James Callaghan has observed (1978, p. A27), "help for the developing countries is not only a moral imperative but, like the Marshall Plan, an act of statemanship and enlightened self-interest." Callaghan goes on to note that "in my country, we have a job of political education to do if we are to convince our own people of the enlightened self-interest of such a policy."

While the economic interdependence of the world's nations is evident, they do not yet have common goals. Thus, economic interdependence is likely to develop only in the face of an imminent danger to the international community—a danger that threatens all countries and can be averted only by a joint effort. But political interdependence is already a reality to the extent that the world is now multipolar instead of bipolar. When approximately 25 countries out of 150 are able to have a significant effect on international affairs, the wishes of the leading powers can be opposed by the weaker states. Thus, not only the humanitarian implications of interdependence but also the realities of international politics require the American people and their government to show greater concern for the rest of the world. Secretary of State Cyrus Vance underscored this point in a speech on May 1, 1979, referring to "the sudden awareness that our economic life can be shaped by actions abroad; and . . . the realization that there are events which affect us but which we can only partly influence" (Vance, 1979).

The high rate of oil consumption in the United States and its impact on the international—as well as the American—economy is but one example of the need for greater appreciation of the interdependence of nations. American oil imports increased from about $5 billion in 1972 to $44.3 billion in 1977;[2] by 1977, nearly half of our oil was imported. Dependence on imported oil was the chief factor in the 1978 trade deficit of $28.5 billion, which weakened the dollar abroad and hampered efforts to deal with unemployment and inflation at home. In its annual report for 1977, the Bank for International Settlements urged the industrialized nations—especially the United States—to reduce their dependence on imported oil because of the depressing effect of balance-of-payments deficits on their economies. Yet according to a Gallup poll reported on April 30, 1978, ten days after the president had announced a national energy conservation program, 40 percent of the American people either did not believe that oil is imported or did not realize the severity of the situation.[3]

Lester Brown (1978), of Worldwatch Institute, has asserted that simpler life-styles and deliberately lower levels of consumption will be necessary if the United States and other affluent nations are to adjust to the earth's limited capacities and resources. On the issue of oil consumption alone, massive

[2]Price increases accounted for $36 billion of this figure.

[3]However, 81.9 percent of college freshmen considered energy conservation the most important issue facing the nation—ahead of the environment, which had been in first place (*Higher Education and National Affairs*, 1978, p. 4).

public education is needed to convince the electorate of the long-term consequences of failing to prepare for the inevitable shrinkage of oil supplies.

New Actors on the World Stage

Not only has the international community become multipolar instead of bipolar; it has greatly expanded and diversified since World War II. More than 90 new states have been created since 1940, for a total of over 150. Among these are nearly 35 with populations of less than 1 million, including 17 "microstates" with fewer than 300,000 inhabitants. While relatively few of these states can affect U.S. interests in any major way, the United States must take their interests and circumstances into consideration. Today, our international concerns and foreign-policy preoccupations extend far beyond those of the cold-war years, when we concentrated on the Soviet Union, Western Europe, and Japan. Now the Third World must be included as well. An aide to President Carter has put it succinctly: "These people have the potential to get America by the throat one day. . . . We want to make sure that they realize it would hurt them as much as us if they ever tried it" (Smith, 1978, p. 14).

There are other actors on the world stage besides the nation-states, including the multinational corporations, whose influence on world affairs is increasing rapidly. Operating large-ly outside the control of national governments, they can achieve enormous economies of scale. On the one hand, they can avoid such local problems as strikes and interest rates; on the other, because of their resources and flexibility, they can compete effectively against local interests. Thus, a few hundred corporations can influence the lives of millions of people, especially people in the developing world, as much as or more than many governments. The international corporations are believed to account for "one-seventh of the world's GNP and $500 billion worth of business" (Hayden, 1977, p. 5).

Also active on the international scene are the international organizations, both public and private—another category of actors whose numbers and concerns have proliferated since World War II. The most visible of these are the United Nations and the many agencies affiliated with it, such as the Food and Agriculture Organization, UNESCO, the World Health Organization, and the World Bank. Many of these agencies, some of which are almost totally unknown to the average American, are concerned with such matters as telecommunications, international trade and finance, maritime law, drug traffic, and human rights. Regional organizations such as the European Economic Community, the Organization for African Unity, and the Organization of American States are other examples of major actors whose activities have reshaped and redefined the concerns and activities of the international community. The number of private or nongovernmental organizations has likewise increased greatly, aided by developments in international travel and communication and spurred by the fact that more and more issues are spilling across national boundaries.

The president of the International Studies Association, Chadwick Alger (1978b), has pointed to another set of entities that are active on the international scene: subnational units. World affairs, broadly defined, are affected not just by nation-states but also by state or provincial governments, cities, religious organizations, private associations and institutions, and the like. Alger urges an approach to international studies that takes into account such entities and enables people "to perceive options for self-conscious participation" in international affairs.

In *People in the Future Global Order* (1978a), Alger expands on what he calls "the disintegrative processes within nation-states" that are changing traditional frameworks for the formulation of foreign policy. According to Alger, national governments cannot adequately serve public needs from a single center because of the growing agenda of social and economic issues. Moreover, subnational units—ranging from the Basques to the International Association of Churches—are demanding participation in the form of ethnic and regional autonomy or direct relations with other countries and their subunits; examples are agreements between the state of Washington and British Columbia and, at another level, between New York City and the United Nations. In addition, new transportation and communication technologies make it easier to establish connections between subnational units. Third-world demands for a greater share of the world's wealth, because of their emphasis on self-reliance and the importance of the local community, also portend a decline in the role of the nation-state. In Alger's words, "The present set of nation-states will not be the exclusive building blocks for the future global order."

An important aspect of these changes is the tension between the internalization of values by the mass media and the trend toward greater national, regional, and even local identity and loyalty. One observer has summarized this situation as follows: "A paradoxical development has taken place in the international community during the 1960s and '70s. Through TV, newspapers, and other media, the average man in the U.S. and elsewhere has had access to more information about the life of his fellow citizens in other countries than ever before. This has however not 'internationalized' people or decreased the emphasis on national cultures and languages to the extent which was once expected. On the contrary, in developing and developed countries alike, the support of indigenous cultures and local languages has gained momentum. The support forms a particularly important part of the nation building in newly independent countries in Africa and elsewhere." This development has important implications, especially for language and area studies, which are treated later in this book.

Cultural Contact and Diversity

Americans will need to become more sensitive to other cultures in the years ahead because they will have more contact with them. There will be, for example, more Americans traveling abroad (7 million in 1977) and, very possibly, more people from foreign countries wanting to study, sojourn, or settle in the United States (22 million in 1979).

Not only will there be increased contact with people of other cultures; there will be more people to come into contact with. The world's population is increasing rapidly; our planet now has 4 billion inhabitants and is becoming more crowded every day. Population expert Roger Revelle predicts an eventual world population of about 50 billion if population growth per-

sists at the rates prevailing in the mid-1970s, but a possible
leveling off at 10 to 12 billion if those rates could be reduced
(American Academy of Arts and Sciences [AAAS], 1978).
According to the United Nations Fund for Population Activities, the rate of population growth is beginning to slow, and it is
possible that by the year 2000 the world's population will be
5.8 billion rather than 6 billion. Of this total, close to 90 percent will be in the developing world. Since the 1960s, birthrates
have fallen by approximately 15 percent in some 40 countries,
and those countries account for about half the population of the
developing world ("U.N. Sees Population Rise Slowing," 1978).
However, even with reduced birthrates, world population growth
will put pressure on the more sparsely populated—and more affluent—countries such as the United States in the years ahead. While
the population explosion does not necessarily mean that there
will be more contact between Americans and people of other
cultures, an increase in such contacts is highly likely.

The expanded international concerns and involvements of
the United States will require more Americans to communicate
with people from other countries and cultures. Some of their
contacts with non-Americans may generate misunderstanding
and resentment. As I will point out later in connection with
general education, an important goal of international education
is to create empathy. In this connection the cultural diversity
within American society, which is more vital today than ever
before, can be a resource for strengthening cross-cultural understanding.

Finally, greater cross-cultural empathy may be required as
a result of increasing numbers of non-Americans coming to this
country. An increase in the emigration of educated people from
the developing world to the United States and other industrialized countries is a very real prospect. Blaug (1977, p. 6)
warns that unemployment is likely to become a major problem
in many developing countries, beginning with India. According
to Blaug, highly educated manpower is being generated "in
most African, Asian, and Latin American countries beyond all
possible hopes of absorbing them in gainful employment." But

trends toward equal educational opportunity make it politically impossible to cut back on higher education in favor of lower levels of the education system. This situation may lead to intensified efforts by educated citizens to find jobs abroad. In addition, despite immigration regulations, the number of non-nationals living in the United States will probably continue to mount, with the "silent invasion" across the Mexican border augmenting the 6 to 12 million "undocumented" or illegal aliens already here. Rising foreign-student enrollments, now an estimated 250,000 and projected at close to 1 million by the end of the 1980s, will also add to the number of non-Americans in the United States, further increasing the need to strengthen cross-cultural education.

Learning from Others

Not only is the United States no longer able to go completely unchallenged in the modern world; other countries may surpass it in particular areas of achievement. In fact, they already have. President Derek Bok of Harvard University emphasized this development in the university's 1975-76 annual report (1977, pp. 30-31):

> It is quite possible that the United States will gradually relinquish its position as the undisputed leader in matters of economic organization and material prosperity. Sweden and Switzerland have already overtaken us in per-capita living standards, and other nations have achieved growth rates that may enable them to equal or surpass us during the next generation. This change in an area of activity where we have long taken our superiority for granted will profoundly affect our sense of ourselves. Although we may react by growing more defensive and insecure, it is more likely that we will respond by becoming more sensitive to the policies and practices of other countries as we search for solutions to the common problems of advanced, industrial societies.

In summary, Americans must achieve a better understanding of the cultures and values of other peoples and possibly learn from them how to find more effective solutions to shared problems. With these goals in mind, American colleges and universities should place a new priority on international education.

2

Recent Social and Educational Changes

American society has changed dramatically since World War II, and so has American higher education. Yet further change is needed. If international education programs are to be effective in the future, they should aim beyond the priorities of the 1950s and 1960s. Those priorities were, for the most part, incorporated into federal legislation (some of which, such as the 1966 International Education Act, was never funded). But in recent years, major changes in the values and composition of society—in the media and in public education generally and in higher education specifically—have altered the needs and prospects for international education.

Before considering these topics, it is important to note that President Carter's appointment of a Commission on Foreign Language and International Studies is itself a reflection of the changing needs in international education. It is one indication of the new role of the United States in the international community—a role requiring that greater priority be given to ensuring an adequate supply of specialists on other countries (for example, the Arab states of the Middle East) and on international issues (for example, energy supplies). The establishment of the commission also indicates the increasingly urgent need for a citizenry that is broadly informed about the rest of the world.

Recent Social Changes

American society today, in contrast to two or three decades ago, is characterized by enhanced consciousness of cultural diversity, higher levels of information and education, and greater commitment to societal participation on the part of young people (although there is considerable ambivalence in this last area). In addition, Americans have greater exposure to other cultures. In 1970, about 17 percent of all Americans were either of foreign parentage or foreign born, and immigration (both legal and illegal) is expected to account for almost half of the nation's population growth between 1970 and 2000. As a result of increases in the Chicano, Cuban, and Puerto Rican populations in the continental United States, this country now has the seventh- or eighth-largest Spanish-speaking population in the world. Also contributing to the cultural diversity of America are blacks (about 11 percent of the population), Asian Americans (2 percent), and many other ethnic groups, mainly of European origin. In 1976, there were 30 million people in the United States whose native tongue was not English or who lived in households where languages other than English were spoken. In short, ethnic and cultural diversity is far from decreasing and may well increase in the future.

Americans' greater consciousness of ethnicity and cultural diversity is part of a worldwide tendency to emphasize their value. Assertion of racial and cultural identity is simultaneously a vehicle for and an obstacle to the internationalization of education. On the one hand, international education programs should encourage and take advantage of cultural diversity because it offers opportunities to work toward better mutual understanding among different groups. On the other hand, cultural and ethnic differences can militate against a national consensus on educational goals.

Another social change that has implications for international education is the increase in female employment. The rate of female participation in the labor force has soared in recent decades, from 18.4 million in 1950 to 40 million in 1977. In only 13 percent of American families does one find the stereotype of "dad the breadwinner, mom the homemaker, and a few kids" (Yankelovich, 1978, p. 2). Most wives now have paid jobs outside the home. If, as various studies suggest, higher family income and increased involvement in the wider society make for greater concern with public issues and more political participation, the higher rate of female employment increases the number of people who are aware that international issues impinge on their lives and, thus, increases the clientele for international education programs.

Among the most dramatic changes in American society in the past 25 or 30 years has been the arrival of television. The percentage of American homes with TV sets increased from 55.7 percent in 1954 to 97.9 percent in 1977, and during this period the average number of hours of TV use per household went up from about 4.5 to over 6 per day (Sterling and Haight, 1978). The role of television in international education is enormously influential. Although American TV is oriented to the American scene, especially in commercial programming, international coverage has improved markedly in recent years.

As TV viewing has increased, newspapers have become less important as sources of public information. The percentage of the population for whom newspapers are the most frequently used source of news declined from 57 percent in 1959 to 49 percent in 1976. Nevertheless, James Reston of the *New York Times* is sanguine about the prospects for serious analytical reporting of international affairs in the press. In his view "there is a new generation of press journalists rising in this country. . . . A thoughtful rising generation of reporters in the press is realizing that they must begin to pay far more attention to the causes of human turmoil and human conflict" (Reston, 1976, pp. 72-73).

Several statements about the effects of these trends on international education can be made. Most Americans spend many hours watching television every week and tend to depend on it for national and world news. Fewer people listen to the radio (and for fewer hours), and newspapers have declined as a source of information about world affairs. The media still neglect news of the non-Western world; but Americans are more aware today than they were 20 years ago of the existence of remote countries and different cultures. However, although Americans are far more familiar with the rest of the world than they used to be, they probably do not understand it any better. They have seen it on TV, and, because more Americans travel abroad, they have seen it (mostly Western Europe) in actuality. The result is a combination of déjà vu and a lack of analytical knowledge and understanding. International-education programs should use the increase in public awareness of the rest of the world as a base for developing a more informed understanding of other countries and of international issues.

Another important change in American society is the increase in people who have gone to college. The percentage of the adult population who had graduated from college increased from 6.2 percent in 1950 to 19 percent in 1973 (Nunn, Crockett, and Williams, 1978). In this connection, it is interesting to note that members of private organizations concerned with world affairs tend to have had at least some college education (Chittick, 1977). The significance of the increase in the number of college-educated Americans has to do with their understanding of and involvement in politics, including international politics. In a study of citizens' propensity to participate in public affairs, Rosenau (1972) reviewed the various factors in people's social backgrounds that correlate with political participation and concluded that "most analysts consider higher education to be most powerful of all the background variables" (pp. 60-61). Thus, it is hardly surprising that, in early 1979, a *New York Times*/CBS News poll showed that college graduates are more favorable toward the SALT negotiations than people with a grade-school education (Clymer, 1979). This finding suggests that more Americans are receptive to international education and concerned about international issues.

American values have also changed in the past two decades, especially among younger people, and they appear to have changed in two somewhat contradictory ways. On the one hand, many people seem to have opted for private values that imply reduced involvement in public affairs; on the other hand, there is evidence of a search for ways to combine concern for personal fulfillment with the desire to participate in and have a lasting impact on society. Yankelovich (1974, p. 6) has elaborated on the new emphasis on self-fulfillment, which he calls "the individual's way of saying that there must be something more to life than making a living, struggling to make ends meet, and caring for others. The self-fulfillment concept also implies a greater preoccupation with self at the expense of sacrificing one's self for family, employer, and community."

Young people are also more concerned about international affairs: In a survey of nearly 2,000 young people aged 14 to 25, three-fourths indicated that "international affairs were *highly important* to their futures" and that they were for the most part "more interested in and knowledgeable about the subject than their teachers" (Kulakow, 1976, p. 8). A comparable national trend was identified by Potomac Associates in a 1976 survey that concluded that "the trend downward along the internationalist/isolationist continuum has probably ceased and is possibly starting to rise. . . . For the present, the jury is still out on whether the public is willing to make any financial sacrifices on the so-called interdependence issues" (Bloomfield, 1976, pp. 9-10). More recently, a public-opinion survey sponsored by the Chicago Council on Foreign Relations, while suggesting that the public is showing greater selectivity with regard to international commitments, also revealed that "willingnesss to strengthen our nation's capacity to defend high priority commitments has increased since 1974" (Rielly, 1979, p. 7).

Countering the increase in concern about international affairs and involvement in public affairs is a growing disenchantment with science, technology, and material progress. In a world where many technological advances endanger the environment and the quality of life, the role of the individual is diminished while anonymity and impotence are intensified. Among the results, according to Nisbet (1977, p. 6), are "the proliferation of occultism, messianism, and pentecostalism, along with other manifestations of the anti- or nonrational [and] . . . the epidemic of obsession with ego or self."

These various ambivalent trends can be harnessed in a positive direction if international education can present issues that are, in Cleveland's words, "actionable" or "concrete enough to affect the lives of identifiable people, and well-managed enough to give them a sense of participation as partners in equality" (1977a, p. 15). International education should avoid dismaying young people with the magnitude and complexity of international issues such as poverty and famine, overwhelming as they are; rather, it should capitalize on students' increased interest in world affairs, emphasizing such issues as how to reduce the birthrate or clean up oil spills.

Changes in Higher Education

Both education and students have changed since the Vietnam War, and they will change even more. The changes have to do with demographic trends, financial pressures, student motivation, diminishing opportunities for graduates, and the definition of "the educated person." More people are getting more education but less assurance that this will lead to employment, and more employed people are seeking postsecondary education. These various developments have several implications for international education.

The decline in the birthrate (from 112.7 births per 1,000 women of childbearing age in 1957 to 68.5 in 1974) portends a major drop in the college-age cohort (although the birthrate apparently is beginning to rise again). It is estimated that the number of 18- to 20-year-olds—and, thus, of college enrollments—may diminish by as much as one fourth over the next 15 years, with the result that new-faculty hiring, which averaged 30,000 per year in the late 1960s, may decline to around 6,000 per year in the 1980s (Ford Foundation, 1977, p. 5). Because the kinds of courses taught at each college or university are determined chiefly by the faculty, the decline in new-faculty hiring will make it increasingly difficult to introduce new subjects. Moreover, the average age of faculty members will rise, as will the percentage who are tenured. It may be very difficult to motivate such faculty to teach courses with an international orientation.

Also working to the disadvantage of international education is the growing vocationalism of higher education. It is
urgent that the so-called vocational subjects be internationalized
and that *vocational* be redefined to include an international
dimension. Concern about the difficulty of finding employment
is propelling students into fields in which job opportunities appear relatively favorable (such as business, engineering, health
services, and other professional fields) and away from the social
sciences and humanities, which have traditionally offered an
international (though rarely non-Western) perspective. The percentage of undergraduate students majoring in these fields declined from 18 and 9 percent, respectively, in 1969 to 8 and 5
percent in 1976 (Carnegie Foundation for the Advancement of
Teaching, 1977). However, students majoring in professional
fields have become more interested in combining them with
international studies. As we will see later, this development
augurs well for internationally oriented professional school programs like those offered by Harvard Law School (which offers
courses in Islamic Law) and the Wharton School (which offers
work on the Middle East as an option in its business administration curriculum).

A major in international studies in the traditional sense is
not usually perceived as a stepping stone to a career (Wiegner,
1978). Therefore, it is not surprising that students increasingly
pursue courses that they believe are likely to lead to jobs and
that they are less willing to take courses in international studies,
despite their intellectual challenge and importance. The Bureau
of Labor Statistics' prediction that 25 percent of those who
graduate from college between 1976 and 1985 will have to
settle for jobs that did not previously require a college degree
suggests the intensity of the competition for jobs among college
graduates.

The job situation is particularly severe for graduate students. In June 1978, about one-fifth of the 31,000 new Ph.D.'s
still did not have jobs. Whereas 50 to 60 percent of new Ph.D.'s
have found jobs in higher education in the past decade, it is now
predicted that only 10 percent will do so in the 1980s and that
barely one-third will find jobs that are related to their post-

graduate education. This competition is not likely to diminish. Despite the decline in the number of federally funded graduate fellowships from about 50,000 in 1968 to fewer than 19,000 in the mid-1970s, some 30,000 new Ph.D.'s are expected to come onto the market annually. In view of recent major cutbacks in private and public funding of international studies, the prospects for graduate study and employment in this field, especially in the academic world, are unfavorable.

Still other trends are reinforcing this "vocational" pressure on higher-education curricula. More students now see higher education as preparation for a job rather than as a foundation for life in all its dimensions; they seek "knowledge for use." The influence of consumerism has encouraged students to demand some assurance that higher education will guarantee them a good job, and the closer relationship between higher education and work has intensified this trend. In this connection, it is worth noting that, in 1977, 36 percent of all degree-credit students were at least 25 years old compared with 28 percent in 1972.[1] Thus, the traditional pattern of first going to college and then finding a job no longer prevails. Students are combining education and work in a variety of ways, and higher education is now expected to meet a wider range of social values, especially job relevance.

Also intensifying the shift toward greater concern with employment is the increase in the percentage of part-time students in postsecondary education. In fall 1977, they accounted for 4.5 million of the 11.4 million students enrolled in degree-credit courses (*Higher Education and National Affairs,* 1978). Because many of these part-time students are either already employed and pursuing postsecondary education in order to improve their employment situation or not employed and hoping to gain better job qualifications, they tend to enroll in courses that are thought to be vocationally useful. A recent study by the College Entrance Examination Board (CEEB) found that some 40 million Americans are undergoing or contemplating job or career

---

[1]A degree-credit student is one who is enrolled in a course (that is, not merely auditing) with the goal of eventually earning a specific academic degree.

changes and that, of these, around 24 million are already engaged in or planning to undertake further training and education. Not surprisingly, these "in-transition" adults are interested in "professional programs or vocational, trade or technical programs" (Arbeiter and others, 1978, p. 21). While the growing pool of older and part-time students may appear to offer a solution to shrinking enrollments, relatively few of these students are likely to enroll in new curricular programs in international education. Once again, this points out the importance of internationalizing existing courses and programs.

Another trend affecting the prospects of international education is the decline in public confidence in higher education. People are no longer as prone to view education as an instrument of social change as they once were. Public funding at both the federal and state levels are therefore unlikely to increase significantly. But if international education is to become a priority, adequate funding must be obtained.

The study of foreign languages can be considered a barometer of interest in international education, although English is widely regarded as a *lingua franca* and foreign-language study may often be simply a matter of course requirements. From this perspective, the decline in foreign-language study augurs poorly for international education and for the international perspective of those who are about to enter the world of work. Foreign-language enrollments declined by nearly 17 percent between 1970 and 1977, and the percentage of college and university students registered in foreign-language courses dropped from 17 percent in 1960 to about 8 percent in 1977 (Scully, 1978). In fall 1978, only 1 percent of entering freshmen expected to major in a foreign language, compared with 2 percent of high school seniors in 1972 (College Entrance Examination Board, 1974, 1978a). However, it is only fair to note that, as suggested earlier, the decline in foreign-language study may say more about curricular requirements than about interest in foreign languages per se; besides, it probably says little about students' actual language proficiency, because relatively few people gain full command of a foreign language by studying it in high school or college.

Offsetting the somewhat dismal prospects described thus far are other, more positive trends. For one thing, there is increased demand for adult education, which includes general education as well as vocational courses. For another, the current shift toward a core curriculum or increased general education requirements in undergraduate programs typically results in the inclusion of international education in one form or another.

On the first point it is estimated that, of the 17 million adults currently engaged in some kind of noncollegiate post-secondary education, one-fourth are enrolled in general-education courses (Coughlin, 1978b). Many Americans enroll in adult education courses in order to be broadly informed and enriched, not just to improve their job qualifications. In one adult-education program that focuses on world affairs—the Great Decisions Program of the Foreign Policy Association—some 100,000 people participate in the eight weekly discussion sessions each year, while an estimated 4 to 6 million listeners follow the discussions on National Public Radio (McDowell, 1978). As with most adult-education programs, the participants have typically had some college education (52 percent compared with 26 percent of the total adult population; Rosenthal, 1977) and tend to be part of the "attentive public."

One form of education that is currently growing at a dramatic rate and has important implications for international education is museum attendance, which in American museums now exceeds 300 million people per year. Special exhibits such as "The Treasures of Tutankhamen" have drawn unprecedented crowds; the 1.3 million who saw the "King Tut" exhibit during its four-month New York run in 1978-1979 were only a small percentage of those who wanted to see it. When local educational institutions make a museum exhibit the focus of a special course, as many did in the case of King Tut, its contribution to international education can be structured and enhanced.

Another trend that is likely to increase interest in international education is the renewed emphasis on course requirements and core curricula in higher-education institutions as well as their greater willingness to define "the educated person." Harvard, for example, recently announced that it will require a core curriculum in its undergraduate program. While Harvard may be considered to be in the forefront of this trend, it is only one of many institutions that are moving in this direction.

The Harvard core curriculum, which will become fully operative in September 1983, sets forth five core areas, one of which relates to foreign languages and cultures: "A Foreign Languages and Cultures requirement in the proposed core is specifically designed to expand the student's range of cultural experience and to provide fresh perspectives on his or her own cultural assumptions and traditions. This aim may be achieved through core courses in Literature and the Arts, History, or Social Analysis, or in special courses in Foreign Languages and Cultures. The intention here is not merely to avoid an exclusive focus on Western traditions but to expose students to the essential and distinctive features of major alien cultures, whether Western or non-Western" (Harvard University, 1978, p. 4).

The Vietnam War and the resulting student protests of the 1960s brought about a decrease in undergraduate course requirements. General-education requirements declined from 43 to 34 percent of the curriculum between 1967 and 1974 (Carnegie Foundation for the Advancement of Teaching, 1977). However, various forces may now be reversing that trend: renewed emphasis on quality in higher education; the need for greater curricular coherence (instead of the "smorgasbord" of unrelated courses offered in recent years); increased concern with humanistic values; and increased emphasis on preparing students to cope with a complex society and a complex world. But given the lack of agreement on what an undergraduate education should consist of in terms of skills and concepts, together with the problems that are inherent in multidisciplinary programs, there is some doubt whether the swing back toward a core curriculum will have much effect on international education.

What we now know about the probable future, both of the United States and the international community, points to the rapidly growing salience of international affairs in the lives of Americans. This situation calls for a far wider understanding of international issues on the part of many more Americans, particularly among those in public and private life who are called upon to deal with these issues. The fact that Americans are more educated today than in the past offers new opportunities for the strengthening of international education. However, a far greater effort is needed than has been undertaken so far. This effort must be directed both toward general education for many students and toward advanced education for a small pool of experts. The following chapters address these parallel needs.

3

International Education at the Undergraduate Level

In an article about the British view of the world, O'Leary (1978, p. 4) writes: "A survey to be published shortly . . . reveals that two-thirds of the nation holds parochial and introverted views and is unsympathetic to a world perspective. 'Attitudes toward the underdeveloped countries in particular are confused by stereotype images, post-colonial guilt, racial and cultural prejudices, limited, unbalanced knowledge, concern about future domestic employment, the belief that overseas development is synonymous only with aid and that aid is motivated only by charity,' the report says." But for the phrase "post-colonial guilt," this excerpt could just as well apply to the United States. Like the United States, Great Britain and some of the other industrialized nations have recently become more aware of the need to strengthen the international component of their educational system. Sweden, for example, is endeavoring to internationalize its entire educational system. In Japan, both the government and the universities are stressing the need to strengthen the international dimension of higher education; among other things, a special Bureau of International Affairs has been established in the Ministry of Education. Great Britain's 1977 Green Paper, "Education in Schools," lists as one of the aims of education "to help children understand the world in which we live, and the interdependence of nations" (Great Britain, 1977, p. 5). It goes on to say, "We . . . live in a complex, interdependent world, and many of our problems in Britain require international solutions. The curriculum should therefore reflect our need to know about and understand other countries."

To achieve this goal, the funding of in-service teacher-education courses dealing with third-world countries and issues is being tripled immediately and will increase to £2.8 million by 1982-83; in addition, new programs to increase public awareness of the Third World are planned (O'Leary, 1978). Britain's Department of Education and Science is also setting up a committee on education for international understanding, partly to encourage schools to promote international education.

This chapter discusses the current situation in international education at the undergraduate level in American colleges and universities and in the secondary schools as a prelude to the collegiate. Subsequent chapters deal with foreign-language study, foreign-student enrollment and programs, overseas study for American students, international faculty exchanges, the involvement of higher education in technical assistance abroad, advanced training and research, and the reinforcement and integration of these activities and programs through more unified or centralized administration.

The Decline in International Studies

Rose L. Hayden of the American Council on Education (n.d., pp. 2-3) has noted that:

> Less than 1 percent of the college-aged group in the U.S. is enrolled in any courses which specifically feature international issues or areas.
>
> While nine out of ten Americans cannot speak a second language, foreign-language enrollments at all levels have dropped. . . . Six of seven junior and community college students are not even exposed to any foreign-language sequence.

Fewer than 5 percent of the teachers being trained today have any exposure whatsoever to international, comparative, area, and other intercultural courses in their work for certification. . . .

A recent survey of civic education reports that 14-year-olds in the U.S. rank near the top among students in eight countries in knowledge of local, state, and national affairs, but next to last in their knowledge of world affairs.

Although some of these statistics are of doubtful validity, the point is well taken: enrollment in and emphasis on international studies are grossly inadequate. To remedy this situation, it will be necessary to undertake a two-pronged effort aimed at general undergraduate education on the one hand and advanced training and research on the other. This effort cannot be merely cognitive but should help Americans appreciate on an affective basis —at the "gut level"—the fact that people in other countries have different values from ours and different attitudes toward issues that affect all of us.

The Schools

Fred Burke, New Jersey Commission of Education, has summarized the current situation in international education as follows: "Not much is going on, and we know very little about that little" (1978, p. 6). What evidence there is suggests that there is much more teaching about the rest of the world available now than there was 30 years ago but probably less than there was 10 years ago.

International education is a low priority in elementary and secondary education. Because of declining enrollments and the consequent reduction in the number of electives available to students, the number of international-studies courses, typically considered "extra," has been reduced. The declining tax base (which threatens to get worse since the passage of California's Proposition 13), makes such courses even more dispensable in the eyes of curriculum planners. Moreover, those planners have other priorities—consumerism, drug abuse, and "back to basics"

—and those priorities do not include foreign-language courses and international studies.

A basic problem with international studies in the schools is its low priority in the eyes of the general public. At the local level, parents, teachers, and principals are not yet persuaded that contemporary social conditions compel greater emphasis on international education. Evoking this essential awareness without some new national or international crisis is a major challenge.

There are several other reasons for the current lack of emphasis on international education. Funding for summer institutes for international-studies teachers has diminished, as has funding for private organizations that have been important in teacher education and in-service training and in international-studies curriculum development. The decline in foreign-language requirements for admission to colleges and universities has taken its toll on foreign-language enrollments in the schools, which have proceeded to drop their own foreign-language requirements. Moreover, the fact that foreign languages often are not taught very well deters students from enrolling in them. The neglect of international studies in the college entrance tests administered by the Educational Testing Service and the American College Testing Service is also a factor in the current situation; and still another is lack of teacher competency in the international field—teachers naturally prefer to teach what they know, and many are inadequately equipped to deal with the rest of the world (although good teaching materials are available). Finally, the foreign-language programs that do exist tend to neglect teaching about other cultures.

Offsetting this dismal scenario are many somewhat isolated and weakly synchronized initiatives to strengthen international education in the schools. Some states are making real efforts in this field, especially those with forceful leadership at the state level and those with some centralization of curriculum planning. Among them are New York, Rhode Island, California, New Jersey, Utah, North Carolina, Illinois, Iowa, and Michigan. It is possible that enough major states are now committed to international education to constitute the beginning of a nationwide trend in this direction.

Ernest Boyer, the former Commissioner of Education, stated more than once that "global education" was one of his several priorities, and since 1977 a Global Education Task Force in the Office of Education (OE) has applied itself to identifying the implications of greater emphasis on global education. Effective January 1, 1979, the American Association of Colleges for Teacher Education (AACTE) formally included multicultural education among the accreditation criteria for its member institutions, which train 95 percent of the school teachers in the United States. Similarly, the Commission on Schools of the North Central Association of Colleges and Secondary Schools, which encompasses 19 states, recently adopted standards for school self-evaluation that include global education; these standards will go into effect in 1980 (Kinghorn, 1978). The Charles F. Kettering Foundation, which supported this initiative, will also support the costs of workshops to provide school principals and teachers with an in-depth understanding of the new program.[1]

A survey prepared in 1975 indicated that, since the late 1960s, progress toward strengthening international education in schools and in teacher training has been mixed (Council of Chief State School Officers [CCSSO], 1976). In terms of curriculum, the record appeared favorable: "Striking new developments are: the growing awareness of the concept of international education; the inclusion of more specific global and international education courses; and the production of social studies and humanities materials dealing with the topic of international education (35 states)" (Hayden, 1976a, p. 5).

In the past few years, various private organizations have been active in developing international education in the schools. Among them are:

1. The Global Development Studies Institute, through its research, teacher workshops, publications, and outreach program.
2. Global Perspectives in Education, which, among other things,

---

[1]The Kinghorn article describes the joint project between North Central and the Charles F. Kettering Foundation that led to the adoption of the evaluation option.

has trained some 3,000 teachers in global education and publishes a teachers' manual in this area called *Intercom*.

3. The Institute for Development of Educational Activities, affiliated with the Kettering Foundation.[2]
4. The Mid-America Center for Global Perspectives in Education, which works closely with educational and citizen groups in Ohio, as in its project "Columbus in the World, The World in Columbus,"[3] and similar projects in Illinois and Indiana (for example, see Mehlinger, 1976).
5. The Center for War/Peace Studies, whose *An Attainable Global Perspective* (Hanvey, 1976) has circulated widely among people who are concerned with global education.
6. The Asia Society in New York.
7. The African-American Institute, through its schools program.
8. The Overseas Development Council of Washington, D. C., which focuses on the developing world.

The efforts of these organizations are impressive and merit significantly more support so that their effects may be extended. This is particularly important because, as Collins (1977, p. 7) has remarked—though with some exaggeration—"approximately 75 percent of the total time and energy devoted to communication of any kind in this field now takes place between a very limited number of individuals located mostly in either the New York City or Washington, D.C., areas."

One of the most effective ways of strengthening international education—the establishment of international schools—is in its infancy in the United States; only a handful of such schools, of which nine are public, are currently in existence. (The private ones tend to have difficulty obtaining adequate funding.) The international school is primarily a European phenomenon, and is illustrated by the school set up in Geneva after World War I for the children of League of Nations personnel

---

[2]See Kinghorn and Shaw (1977), *Handbook for Global Education: A Working Manual*, published by the Kettering Foundation for use mainly by educators working in kindergarten through twelfth grade.

[3]See also Alger (1978a, 1978b) and Alger and Hoover (1978).

and by other such schools established more recently for the "Euro-children" of the European Economic Community staff. The international school gives its pupils a thorough knowledge of other cultures as well as proficiency in at least two languages. It thus offers a model for the strengthening of international studies and foreign-language teaching in American schools.

Other means for strengthening international education, especially foreign-language teaching in the schools, are the "magnet school system" and the introduction of the International Baccalaureate. In the magnet school system, a selected school emphasizes a particular teaching method or a certain curricular theme and enrolls students from a wider area than the local district. It attracts students who are highly motivated to enter a given field and may permit higher achievement in that field than normally occurs. Magnet schools that concentrate on foreign languages circumvent the deterrents of weak motivation, uneven teaching quality, and slow progress toward proficiency.

The International Baccalaureate, a program for able high school students, requires an emphasis on foreign-language study as well as international studies in literature and history. Begun in 1970 in the U.S. in an attempt to create a core curriculum for some of the world's top private schools, the I.B. has been seized upon by public high schools as part of their effort to counter allegations that their academic standards are too low.

The tremendous increase in international study, travel, and teaching by American teachers has strengthened international education by enhancing the competence and motivation of teachers. The fact that more than half of the social studies teachers surveyed in the fall of 1974 had traveled abroad in at least one country testifies to the mobility of teachers in this field (Pike and Barrows, 1976). The 22,380 teachers (7,802 American, 14,578 foreign) exchanged between 1949 and 1975 under the Fulbright-Hays Act (Board of Foreign Scholarships, 1976) are only the tip of the iceberg, because most American teachers going abroad are financed by their school districts and their own resources.

The OE's curriculum-consultants program, though modest

in scope, has contributed to curricular development in international fields. Between 1954 and 1975, this program brought 189 foreign-curriculum consultants to state departments of education, school systems, and teacher-education programs, as well as to groups of community colleges and other higher-education institutions in the United States. Another Fulbright program—Group Projects Abroad, which supports teacher training, research, and curricular development abroad—sent 5,892 teachers and other educational personnel to foreign countries in the 1964-1975 period (Board of Foreign Scholarships, 1976). Unfortunately, OE has not been able to evaluate either the curriculum-consultants program or Group Projects Abroad, but an evaluation of the teacher exchange is to be completed in 1979.

The overall balance sheet for international studies in America's schools is uneven. Public apathy and competing demands, along with financial constraints, stand in the way of a major effort to improve the situation. But a variety of scattered initiatives by a few individuals and organizations are worth noting. In the United States, the major responsibility for educational change rests primarily with the nation's 16,000 school districts. Nevertheless, leadership at the national and state levels is also crucial. If the people who can most directly affect education in primary and secondary schools are to make international education a major priority, its importance must be stressed at the highest levels of government.

Even though it may be extremely difficult to strengthen international education at the school level, it is at this level that the effort is most important. As Reischauer puts it (1973, p. 139), "Something as basic as a sense of world citizenship is probably formed either early in life or not at all." This view is supported by Buergenthal and Torney (1976, p. 122): "Research . . . shows that positive national identity is established very early and forms part of the child's *perspective* for viewing the activity of other nations and of his own, as well as the future of international society. The period before the age of 14 is especially important because the child's openness to diversity in this period is more likely to foster positive international *attitudes.*"

Higher Education

Twenty-five years ago, international studies figured little in American higher education. In 1959, the Ford Foundation launched a $7 million undergraduate program that involved more than 100 colleges and had faculty training as its main target.[4] Undergraduate studies were emphasized because they could reach large numbers of students and make them more aware of the world beyond our national boundaries. Other goals of the program were to modify the concept of undergraduate liberal education to include more non-Western and international studies and to recruit more specialists in area and international studies, since those students who pursue area-studies programs as undergraduates are the ones most likely to do so at the post-baccalaureate level.

International studies have made impressive progress in the past 20 years, though they still have a long way to go. As Lambert noted in his major study (1973, p. 1), "Thirty years ago the American scholarly experts on many of the world areas could have been assembled in a small conference room and . . . today all the world areas are represented by flourishing scholarly associations with memberships running, in some cases, into the thousands." The base for undergraduate international studies may now sufficiently meet the current level of demand. What is urgently needed is a major expansion in the *demand* for international studies. More students should be attracted to international studies, and an international component should be included in courses that have not traditionally been part of international-studies programs. To accomplish this, more faculty trained in international studies or in international aspects of their disciplines are needed. In addition, existing faculty should have many more opportunities to revitalize their international expertise. In short, faculty competence and experience should be internationalized. Among the ways in which this may be accomplished are the following:

[4]The Ford Foundation did not intentionally neglect this area in the early years of its International Research and Training Program; rather, it did not support international studies at the undergraduate level until 1959 because it had not yet developed the necessary faculty expertise and research capacity.

1. Offering more institutions and seminars like those sponsored by the National Endowment for the Humanities, which extend the international education expertise of existing faculty. Colleges and universities should give higher priority to faculty participation in such programs.
2. The introduction of "new math" some years ago provides a model for strengthening international education; namely, federal funding for the preparation of new curricular materials and special seminars to retrain teachers to teach new curricula. Using this model, international education could be integrated into a wide range of disciplines.
3. Because overseas experience offers a unique opportunity to increase faculty competence in international education, opportunities to teach and do research abroad should be increased significantly.
4. Colleges and universities should support international education by providing released-time and professional-growth grants to selected faculty members in order specifically to expand their international experience and expertise.

Enrollment in International Studies

It is virtually impossible to obtain reliable statistics on undergraduate enrollments in international-studies courses. However, a rough approximation can be achieved by estimating the numbers of undergraduates in area or international-studies programs funded by OE. This is an index of students who are not majoring in these fields but are taking courses in them; most undergraduates in these programs do not intend to specialize in area or international studies (Lambert, 1973, p. 239). The place given to international studies in the community and state colleges can also be roughly estimated.[5]

Before these estimates are presented, however, the recent blossoming of "peace studies" should be noted. These programs became popular in the post-Vietnam-War period. Approxi-

---

[5]There is some overlap between undergraduate enrollments in OE-funded international-studies programs and international-studies enrollments in community and state colleges, because OE funds some programs at the latter institutions.

mately 500 colleges and universities now offer such programs, and an estimated 60 undergraduate and 25 graduate programs offer minors or majors in this field. The programs tend to be interdisciplinary and to deal with such issues as hunger, resource allocation, and human rights. Students who are attracted to peace studies are typically planning careers in law, foreign service, labor relations, and the like.

NDEA TITLE VI AREA CENTERS

Because of restrictions imposed by the Office of Management and Budget in 1972 on gathering enrollment data, OE is unable to provide statistics on undergraduate enrollment in NDEA Title VI area centers.[6] Although the number of baccalaureate degrees awarded to students in Title VI area-center programs says little about undergraduate enrollment in international studies as a whole, it is nevertheless of interest that between 1959 and 1976, over 63,000 baccalaureate degrees were awarded to students in Title VI area-center programs with at least 15 credit hours in language and area training (U.S. General Accounting Office, 1978b).

Extrapolating from data in the remarkable Lambert report (1973), as many as 600,000 undergraduates, or around 7 percent of the total, may have been enrolled in 1970 in area-studies courses or in courses with an international component. This estimate is based on an undergraduate enrollment of about 230,000 in foreign-area and language courses offered by the 203 area centers and programs that were qualified to request National Defense Foreign Language (NDFL) Fellowships (Lambert, 1973). This figure is multiplied by a factor of 2 to 3 to include enrollment in Western European studies (which are not included in the Lambert figure) and estimated enrollments in the courses taught by specialists in area studies who teach elsewhere than in the NDFL centers (49.3 percent of the total).

Although some of these students were engaged in specialized training, most were enrolled for general education pur-

---

[6]National Defense Education Act of 1958, Title VI on Foreign Studies and Language Development.

poses. The figure of 600,000 does not take into account students in international-relations courses as contrasted to area courses; nor does it include foreign-language enrollments outside of area-studies programs—some 900,000 in 1970. If these students are included, the percentage of American undergraduates in international-studies courses might have been over 15 percent in 1970. However, it is probably lower today because of cutbacks in Title VI centers from 107 in 1969-70 to 50 in 1973-74 (but back up to 80 since 1976-77) as well as reduced enrollments in foreign-language courses, presumably lower enrollments in international and area-studies courses generally, fewer course offerings, and a diversion of faculty resources away from the international field.

NDEA TITLE VI INTERNATIONAL-STUDIES PROGRAMS

NDEA Title VI has stimulated new and in many cases innovative programs in international studies at the undergraduate level since 1972, when the law was redefined to include undergraduate programs. Under Title VI, the Commissioner of Education may award grants to institutions of higher education or consortia of such institutions "to assist them in providing an effective international perspective to the undergraduate general education program, particularly in the first two years of postsecondary study." The criteria for selection include such factors as the "international nature, contemporary relevance, and interdisciplinary and comparative dimensions of the program," as well as such concerns as institutional commitment to international studies and the replicability of a given program at other institutions.

NDEA Title VI programs are normally funded by OE's Division of International Education for two years (up to three years for consortia). About 12 to 14 new awards are made each year of up to $45,000 for single institutions and $70,000 for consortium programs. In 1978-79, the allocation for all programs was $875,000. Between 1972 and 1979, about $6.5 million went to support undergraduate international-studies programs at 125 colleges, universities, and consortia (U.S. Department of Health, Education, and Welfare, 1978b). The number of students involved in these programs is not known because of Office of Management and Budget restrictions on collecting enrollment data. However, the Office of Education has estimated the numbers of students benefiting from these programs: 60,000 in 1974-75, 86,000 in 1975-76, and 64,000 in 1976-77.

Since 1972, NDEA international-studies programs have been modified to take account of several trends in American higher education: the difficulty of obtaining funding for programs that involve major new departures; diminished faculty recruitment (which means that fewer junior faculty members are granted tenure); the renewed emphasis on training in basic skills; and the decline in resources for higher education in general. The programs that are funded tend to emphasize general education, a mix of disciplines, closer links between academic programs, career training and experience, a focus on major world issues, and the tapping of available resources (for example, the use of foreign students to give a cross-cultural dimension to freshman English courses).

The NDEA programs constitute only a small fraction of all undergraduate international-studies programs in the United States, and over the past seven years they have affected only about 3 percent of American colleges and universities. Yet these programs have been important, especially because the financial resources of higher-education institutions have been diminishing and the funding of international studies from private outside sources, notably foundations, has declined sharply. The relatively minor extent of the various programs funded by Title VI shows that substantially increased funding is needed to strengthen undergraduate international studies—to develop curricular materials, expand library holdings, provide released time for faculty, subsidize faculty travel and summer stipends, and provide honoraria and stipends for outside consultants and visiting scholars. The limited scope of the NDEA program is also evidenced by its staffing: For several years this consisted of one half-time position in the International Studies Branch of the Division of International Education (staffing was increased slightly in 1979). Current staffing does not permit follow-up studies of the programs funded, which presumably would be important in evaluating what, if any, impact they have after OE funding ends. To make possible a regular evaluation of these and other OE programs, the staffing of the Division of International Education should be increased.

NDEA Title VI support of undergraduate international studies is not limited to undergraduates enrolled in courses offered by Title VI programs and centers. The "outreach" activities of Title VI graduate centers (which stem from the requirement that these centers devote the equivalent of at least 15 percent of the funds awarded to them to such activities) also often involve undergraduates. While much outreach activity is aimed at schools, many centers sponsor lectures, colloquia, conferences, summer workshops, and media productions, and these enhance undergraduate education (Mehlinger, 1976). Although the effectiveness of outreach activities varies, some of them have been extremely dynamic in linking center expertise with school and community needs.

State Colleges and Universities

In the state colleges, too, international programs have made progress in recent years. A 1975 survey of international/intercultural education in the 324 members of the American Association of State Colleges and Universities (AASCU) revealed a noteworthy advance since surveys in the 1960s. According to a 1966 study, only 50 percent of the 191 state colleges and universities surveyed offered a course in non-Western studies. The 1975 survey concluded that since the earlier study, "approximately twice as many colleges . . . have developed international curriculum" (Gray, 1977, p. 17).

The 1975 study underscored the difficulty of effecting major change in the curricular programs that are most likely to involve large numbers of students. It documented progress in foreign-student enrollments, overseas study by state-college students, and research and teaching abroad by state-college faculty. But even admitting that state colleges and universities place less emphasis on liberal education than less professionally oriented institutions, the percentage of their students who enroll in international-studies courses is low; moreover, other courses offered by these institutions rarely approach their subject matter from an international perspective. This makes it all the more important to internationalize curricula, a goal to which the AASCU is committed.

Teachers' Colleges

A major study of teacher-education programs published in 1973 by the American Association of Colleges for Teacher Education (AACTE) made the following statement: "It is conceivable that the guestimate [*sic*] made by Harold Taylor in 1968 that *only 3 to 5 percent of prospective teachers had any international preparation* is equally true today" (Klassen, Imig, and Yff, 1973, p. 2.7). The italicized portion of this statement is often quoted, but when it is taken out of context it is extremely misleading. The study did not present as negative a picture as this statement suggests.

The study was conducted by means of a questionnaire sent to 1,000 colleges and universities that prepare and/or retrain educational personnel (and in many cases overlap with the state colleges); 530, or 53 percent, of the institutions responded. The responses showed that the general, or academic, studies that constitute 60 to 80 percent of a prospective teacher's academic program "provide the major educational resource today for incorporating an international dimension in teacher education. During the five-year period 1966-71, over 80,000 education students participated. Approximately 8 percent of today's teachers have had the opportunity to study cultures and concepts on an international plane." (Klassen, Imig, and Yff, 1973, p. 3.7).[7] The study went on to state that 132 of the responding institutions offered "required and elective courses under the general rubric of comparative education." It emphasized that programs of study and teaching abroad, widely perceived as "the most effective and lasting [international] experience both cognitively and attitudinally" were offered, respectively, by 192 and 70

---

[7]A more reasonable estimate of the percentage of students participating is closer to 15 percent; but even 15 percent is grossly inadequate.

institutions (Klassen, Imig, and Yff, 1973, pp. 3.7-3.8). (No figures were given for students participating in these programs.)

It should be noted that the AACTE works actively to strengthen international and intercultural education in teachers' colleges. As already mentioned, as of January 1, 1979, new accreditation requirements for those institutions include multicultural education. Another important step, which remains to be taken, is to make international studies a requirement for teacher certification.

Community Colleges

The extent to which community colleges are internationalized is important in assessing the current state of international education, because over one-third of all degree-credit students in higher education attend community colleges, and over 50 percent of first-year students enter these colleges (Hansen and Gladieux, 1978). A survey of the catalogs of about 50 community colleges scattered throughout the United States found that "in general the community colleges offer very little in the field of international studies" (Chyter, 1977, p. 2). While they offer certain basic courses that deal with the world outside the United States—mainly in history, foreign languages, and political science—few other internationally oriented courses are offered. A student earning an associate degree in business, technical training, nursing, or secretarial science may receive no exposure whatsoever to international issues. The survey concluded that "international studies has not yet found its place in America's community colleges, a situation not unique to these colleges."

Similarly, a 1977 survey of community colleges in Massachusetts (Kelleher, 1977, p. 7) found that "course offerings in international studies, even if defined broadly, seem random at best, with some colleges faring much better than others. Curricula depend on the individual background and proclivities of faculty members and not on a planned program. . . . If the international-studies educational goal is to give a smattering of information to a few students, this is achieved by the present system. . . . If the goal is to reach the general student population, this is simply not being accomplished, nor is it being considered by most of the community college personnel. The potential to reach a sizable number of the general population served by the community college system is there, but it is not being realized."

In contrast, a 1976 study of some 500 two-year colleges (Shannon, 1978; undertaken by the late Horace H. Smith, whose untimely death prevented its completion as initially conceived) indicated that those colleges offered an average of 38 international-intercultural courses, which were attended by 28.7 percent of all two-year college students. Even if these calculations were off by 50 percent, extrapolating the data to all of higher education would result in a figure of 6.3 percent.

International education in community and other two-year colleges seems likely to expand. Since 1975, an International/ Intercultural Community College Consortium, with more than 80 members, has been in existence. The theme of its January 1979 conference was "Internationalizing the Community College." The American Association of Community and Junior Colleges (AACJC) has given significantly higher priority to international education in the past several years and has sponsored a number of special conferences on such subjects as foreign students,[8] study abroad, and internationalizing the curriculum. In 1978, it received a two-year Ford Foundation grant that enabled it to establish the position of Director of International Services at its central office. The AACJC's international commitment was further demonstrated by its choice of Secretary of State Vance as the keynote speaker at its 1979 annual conference.

Another contribution to international education in community colleges is made by projects funded under Title VI. One of these projects is notable in that it offers a model for strengthening international education in a group or system of colleges. The project, which affects all 15 public community colleges in Massachusetts, provides faculty training in developing curricular modules on international topics. Virtually all of the academic

---

[8]These resulted in the publication *The Foreign Student in United States Community and Junior Colleges* (College Entrance Examination Board, 1978b).

disciplines offered by the community college system are represented, from allied health and secretarial programs to history
and literature. Because it adds new material and modules to
existing courses rather than requiring the initiation of new
courses, this project is an exceptional and practical example of
curricular reorientation.

Other Programs and Prospects

Existing federal legislation authorizes international-education
programs for students of all kinds at all levels in both formal
and nonformal education. Under Section 603 of NDEA Title
VI, adopted by Congress in 1976, "the Commissioner is authorized, by grant or contract, to stimulate locally designed
educational programs to increase the understanding of students
in the United States about the cultures and actions of other
nations in order to better evaluate the international and domestic impact of major national policies" (U.S. Dept. of Health,
Education, and Welfare, May 12, 1978a, p. 20496). This legislation permits expanded international-education programming in
postsecondary institutions as well as other organizations and
agencies, such as teachers' organizations; state and local educational bodies; professional associations; and community, adult,
and continuing-education programs.

Under present legislation, no funds can be authorized for
Section 603 until the traditional components of Title VI (Sections 601 and 602) receive appropriations of at least $15 mil-
lion. The purpose of this "trigger clause" is to ensure minimal
funding for existing centers. To that extent, therefore, those
existing centers are removed from competition with the international-education programs of schools and community/adult-
education organizations. The reauthorization of NDEA Title VI
has prompted proposals that the "trigger" be eliminated. However, in view of the importance of such a decision and the fact
that the president's commission is currently studying Title VI, it
would seem inappropriate for the administration to decide to
remove the trigger before the commission has completed its
work.

In the spring of 1979, OE issued a policy statement and

guidelines for grant applications under Section 603. These were to apply to the $2 million allocated to this program for fiscal year 1979, thus leaving open the possibility that the recommendations of the president's commission might affect educational policy in future years. The program will provide about 10 major grants of approximately $100,000 each for teacher retraining. In addition, some four to six mid-level grants of about $80,000 each and 20 to 24 mini-grants of approximately $25,000 each will be awarded to school-based community programs with the goals of increasing citizen awareness of international issues, convincing school personnel of the importance of an international perspective, encouraging schools to use foreign students as a resource, and supporting media programs related to international education.

Still another legislative authority that would permit more federal funding in international education is the Special Projects Act (Section 402 of PL 93-380). It authorizes grants and contracts for special projects, including new efforts in international education.

In general, undergraduate international studies have suffered a decline. The widespread abolition of foreign-language and other course requirements in the late 1960s had a tremendous impact on enrollments in international-studies courses. Indeed, the reduction in course requirements generally has resulted in a sizable reduction in general-education and "civilization" courses. Humanities enrollments have decreased, and along with lower enrollments has come a reduction in the ability of colleges and universities to support international-studies courses. However, there is growing interest in international studies on the part of students in professional schools as well as those preparing for graduate work in business and law or for graduate programs combining international and professional studies. NDEA Title VI centers have been urged to strengthen their staff capacity in order to be in a position to advise the increasing number of students interested in this field (Ellison, 1977).

The reluctance of colleges and universities to recognize international education as a professional priority, together with their failure to emphasize any teaching and research that does not center on a particular discipline, may be the most intractable obstacle to the strengthening of international education. Few of the issues confronting the international community can be defined by a single discipline, but faculty reward systems—especially in recent years—have been defined along single-discipline lines. Also, interdisciplinary studies have long been regarded as lacking the scholarly rigor of the individual disciplines, even though many national and international issues could benefit from an interdisciplinary approach. (The problem of "desertification," for example, is increasingly being treated as a social problem rather than simply a matter of changing climatic conditions. Comprehensive study of this problem field involves geology, sociology, economics, and other disciplines.) The structure of knowledge in institutions of higher education does not correspond to the current need for teaching and research on such issues (Rosenau, 1971). Moreover, the inter- and intrainstitutional competition for students, measured in full-time enrollment equivalents (FTEs),[9] increasingly deters faculty from teaching outside their own departments; if they do, the administration may cut their departments' budgets on the basis of apparently shrinking departmental FTEs.

In this connection, a project of the Council on Learning, "Education and the World View," should make an important contribution. Supported by the National Endowment for the Humanities, it will assess the global perceptions of American college seniors and recommend changes in college curricula. A survey, to be developed and administered by the Educational Testing Service, will focus on college students' knowledge and understanding of world issues and their proficiency in French, Spanish, and Russian. In the words of the project proposal (Council on Learning, 1977, p. 18), "Such a study of today's college seniors is now indicated—to develop hard data, to contribute to the national forum, to pinpoint areas of the curriculum in need of special attention, and to help develop an articu-

---

[9]An FTE may be defined as one student enrolled in one course. Departments are awarded faculty and graduate students on this basis.

late plan for curriculum policy that will influence scholars, administrators, teachers, and political leaders responsible for educational policy across the nation." The project will also include a national invitational conference on "Education and the World View" following the preparation of the final report on the survey, the publication of a special issue of *Change* on the same topic, and the preparation of a *Curriculum Book on Internationalizing Studies* that will "offer a variety of academic disciplines the vision and techniques by which undergraduate offerings can be made culturally more multidimensional" (Council on Learning, 1977, p. 43).

Two relatively recent developments give cause for optimism about the future of international education. The International Communication Agency (ICA), which amalgamated the former U.S. Information Agency and the Department of State's Bureau of Educational and Cultural Affairs and was launched on April 3, 1978, has a new mandate to increase the American people's knowledge and understanding of other countries. According to President Carter, its task is "to assist individual Americans and institutions in learning about other nations and their cultures" (ICA, 1978, p. 24). While it is not yet clear how it will go about this task (it started by assessing the international-education activities carried out by nonprofit, nonacademic organizations and associations), the unmet needs in higher education are so great that ICA should, in partnership with OE, direct some of its efforts toward the millions of Americans enrolled in colleges and universities, expanding and building on educational exchanges to do so.

The increasing support of international education (mainly international studies) by the National Endowment for the Humanities (NEH) is also a promising development. Under the NEH's Fellowships Program, which supports independent study and research in the humanities, 68 percent of the academic-year fellowships and 44 percent of the summer fellowships granted for 1977-78 were for international study. Particularly encouraging is the number of grants made in this field through the NEH's Public Programs Division. These grants went up from 8.79 percent of the total in 1976 to 19.48 percent for the first

nine months of 1978 (NEH, 1978). This increased public interest augurs well for the strengthening of international
education both in higher education and in American society
as a whole.

4

Foreign-Language Study

The decline in foreign-language study in secondary and higher education has become a subject of increasing concern during the past few years. Registrations in foreign-language courses in colleges and universities dropped nearly 19 percent between 1968 and 1977, from about 15 percent of all degree-credit students to 9 percent. Foreign-language enrollments in public secondary schools dropped from 4.75 million in 1968 to 4 million in 1974. Indeed, nearly one-fifth of these schools offer no foreign language at all (information from Modern Language Association).

Many reasons are proffered for this decline: poor teaching, especially at the high school level; the dropping of foreign languages—along with many other traditional fields of study—from the requirements for a college degree; the decrease in Europe's influence on the United States; American parochialism—the assumption that, if English is a leading world language (second only to Mandarin Chinese in number of speakers), then English speakers need speak no language but their own; and finally, the declining number of jobs for people who specialize in foreign languages, especially teaching jobs.

Although federally funded bilingual-education programs offer new job opportunities for foreign-language specialists, mainly in Spanish, so far this has not had an appreciable effect on the job market for linguists. In this connection, and contrary to popular belief, bilingual teaching is not staffed mainly by teachers with appropriate ethnic backgrounds. According to Josué Gonzalez, Director of OE's Office of Bilingual Education, fewer than one-half of all bilingual-program teachers have an ethnic background corresponding with the language they teach. Further, the increasing recognition of the multilingual nature of American society is not reflected in job opportunities for linguists in nonteaching fields. For example, only around 8,000 jobs in the U.S. government (5,500 at high levels) require foreign-language proficiency. As these are easily filled by members of the language group in question, especially Hispanics, the existence of these jobs offers little inducement to college students with non-Hispanic backgrounds to study foreign languages.

Poor teaching may be responsible for the fact that the majority of foreign-language students show little or no proficiency in the language; but what appears to be a result of poor teaching may often be a product of too little teaching and too short an exposure to the language. The Carnegie Council's *Handbook on Undergraduate Curriculum* (Levine, 1978, p. 64) stated that in 1976, 78 percent of college freshmen had taken at least one year of foreign language in high school but that "only 15 percent said their high school programs prepared them very well in foreign languages." The American Council on Education came up with similar findings for 1977: Only 14.3 percent of the college freshmen surveyed could actually speak a second language (Astin, King, and Richardson, 1978). An authority on comparative educational achievement, Torsten Husèn, observed that "in the United States, where French at the high school level as a rule is taken for only two years, the level of competence achieved is rather dismal" (1977, p. 137). Finally, a Ford Foundation report stated that "the principal obstacle to the development of first-class competence in the foreign and international field is the low level of language teaching in the United States" (Swayzee, 1967, p. 56), and it is likely that this is still the case.

Clearly, more teaching as well as better teaching is needed. Levine (1978, p. 64) observes correctly that "in general the students with the most foreign language experience in high school are most likely to take foreign language in college." Taken by itself, this is encouraging for foreign-language study, but it should be noted that fewer than one in twenty recent high school graduates have studied any foreign language more than two years (Starr, 1978b).

Measuring Language Competence

It is misleading to measure the study of languages in terms of years or semesters rather than in terms of specific goals or abilities or, in Hayden's words, to "confuse credentials with competencies" (1976b, p. 16). The Foreign Service Institute of the Department of State is unique in focusing on competence as a measure of language study; the institute is working with nine higher-education institutions to develop criterion-referenced tests of language proficiency that can be used at this level. These tests, while very promising, are still in the developmental stage.

Recognizing the difficulty of assessing the results of foreign-language teaching, the Modern Language Association (MLA) has recommended the development of an outline of realistic proficiency goals by stage of achievement. According to its Task Force on the Commonly Taught Languages (1978a, p. 3; to be described in more detail later), "The sequential nature of many aspects of foreign-language study makes it possible to identify the various stages in the student's acquisition of basic language skills. Unfortunately, current practice provides no clear definition of what these stages are or when they are reached. It is usually impossible to interpret with any accuracy the level of achievement after 'first-year French' or 'third-year Russian,' given the wide range of courses taught under such headings."

The solution to the problem of poor teaching, then, may be found in the development of specific goals together with the recognition that real proficiency in a language cannot be achieved in one or two years of study. It will be necessary to reach a consensus on the aims and priorities of foreign-language study, on precisely what should be accomplished by language programs and courses. At a minimum, there should be a national policy endorsing the principle that every pupil should have an opportunity to learn a foreign language. And foreign-language instruction should be geared to realistic, competency-based learning outcomes that permit (1) better articulation between language programs in secondary and postsecondary education and (2) more effective instructional methods and strategies.

Deterrents to Foreign-Language Study

The dropping of foreign-language requirements for admission to or graduation from college is widely recognized as a major problem, but it may be remedied as colleges return to more structured curricula. From 1966 to 1974, the percentage of colleges and universities with language requirements for admission decreased from 33.6 percent to 18.6 percent, bringing about a corresponding decrease in foreign-language study in high schools. The percentage of institutions with foreign-language requirements for graduation decreased from 89 percent to 53 percent in the same period (Caroux, 1977). Among the colleges and universities that have "distribution" requirements (approximately 60 percent of the total), only 39 percent include foreign language (Levine, 1978).

Moreover, as fewer secondary school students study foreign languages and the number of students in college decreases, jobs for teachers of foreign languages are becoming scarce, thus further discouraging foreign-language study (Coughlin, 1978a). This vicious circle can be broken, however. The recent trend toward restoring distribution requirements should benefit foreign languages as well as other areas of study; this, in turn, should increase foreign-language study in secondary schools and eventually generate new openings for teachers of foreign languages.

Because foreign-language instruction is offered primarily by high schools as part of their general-education curriculum, it is in the high schools that efforts to improve language teaching should be concentrated. In addition, special magnet schools focusing on foreign-language learning might well be established in large school districts. As suggested earlier, such schools could serve as centers for innovation in high school foreign-language study. Moreover, international schools should receive more encouragement and support because of their special contribution to foreign-language learning as well as international education.

As part of such an endeavor, instruction in major world languages that are currently taught to very few students at any level—Chinese, Arabic, Russian, and Japanese—should be more widely available. Also, research is needed on the effectiveness of initiating foreign-language instruction in elementary schools and on the contribution of foreign-language study to the acquisition of linguistic and reasoning skills.

An aspect of foreign-language learning that has attracted relatively little attention until recently is attrition of foreign-language skills. People typically forget much of a foreign language, especially if they were exposed to it only for a year or two, as is normally the case in schools and colleges. Thus, the foreign-language crisis in the United States is not only that few people study foreign languages and few of them gain proficiency in those languages, but also that few of the people who study a language retain much of what they learn.

Politics and economics have an important effect on foreign-language study. As Europe's influence on the United States has diminished, the study of European languages has appeared less important. Nevertheless, in the fall of 1977, 85 percent of the foreign-language registrations in colleges and universities were in European languages—French, German, Italian, and Spanish (Brod, 1978, table 4.1)—with the non-European or "less commonly taught" languages accounting for only 15 percent, despite the significance of those languages in terms of world population. For example, although Indonesia is a major nation with a population of approximately 140 million, only 127 American college and university students were studying Indonesian in 1977 ("The Geography of Languages," 1978). Comparable figures exist for the study of most of the world's non-European languages.[1]

---

[1]Of the estimated 300 separate world languages, 17—spoken by four-fifths of the world's population—have over 50 million native speakers each; but the number of American college students enrolled in them in 1977 bore little relationship to the populations speaking them. The numbers of students enrolled in them in fall 1977,

American parochialism and ethnocentrism lie behind both the decreased interest in European languages and the shocking neglect of non-European ones. There seems to be no practical incentive for the English speaker to learn a foreign language when English is the native language of an estimated 374 million people and is also the official or semiofficial language of 40 countries in which it is not the native language; these countries have a combined population of over 700 million. Moreover, English is the principal language taught in non-English-speaking countries. In France, the percentage of secondary-school students who chose English as their first—or only—foreign language rose from 76 percent in 1958 (465,000) to 81 percent in 1976 (2,681,000) (Cellard, 1977). In the Federal Republic of Germany, 98 percent of all school children choose English as their first foreign language. Regarding the American scene, Grant (1978, p. 10) writes:

> At one time in this country, it was the assumption that a person was not truly educated unless he knew at least one foreign language. Today, not only has that assumption seemed to fade, but the desire to learn another language has also waned. In various ways the need to know languages other than English may be diminishing. For some of the most important fields of human endeavor—science, technology, military affairs, commerce, and finance—English is probably more of a "universal language" than Latin or French has been in the past. English-speaking people in the U.S. often have an almost arrogant attitude toward other languages; the feeling is that others should and must know English to get along in this world. Unhappily, the requirement to teach and to

excluding England and in order of decreasing number of native speakers, were as follows: Mandarin, 9,809; Spanish, 376,697; Russian, 27,784; Bengali, 7; Hindi (with Urdu), 355; Arabic, 3,070; Portuguese, 4,954; Japanese, 10,721; German, 135,371; Wu (Shanghai), no figures given; Italian, 33,327; Javanese, 2; French, 246,115; Telegu, 12; Cantonese, 97; and Korean, 163 ("The Geography of Languages Taught at U.S. Colleges," 1978).

learn foreign languages in the U.S. schools disappears
as the need to know them lessens.

The dominance of English over other languages may not be
permanent, however. Starr (1978a) has noted the low birthrate
of English-speaking peoples and the diminishing status of
English in countries that formerly were colonies—with English
as their official language—but are now independent and seek an
independent identity—of which their own language is an essential part. Although TV and other media provide more information about other countries than ever before, emphasis on national cultures and languages, far from decreasing, has gained
momentum in developing and developed countries alike.

As higher-education systems expand in third-world countries, more third-world students may decide against studying in
England or the United States. This would mean that more
books and textbooks would be published in other languages and
proportionately fewer in English. Starr admits that both the
timing and rate of the decline in the importance of English are
matters of speculation, but he predicts that the future will see
"a world of linguistic egalitarianism" (1978, pp. 26-31). Hap-
pily, a recent report from the Comptroller General shows an
increase in enrollments in the "less commonly taught" languages at postsecondary institutions, from 12,099 in 1960 to
64,071 in 1974 (U.S. General Accounting Office, 1978b).

The linguistic parochialism of Americans is deplorable, but
foreign-language study has declined in other countries too. The
number of British secondary school students taking A-level
French, German, and Spanish fell by almost one-third between
1970 and 1975 ("Scandinavian Hornet's Nest," 1977, p. 28).
Non-European languages suffer the same neglect in Great Britain
as in the United States, a situation that is reflected in enrollments.
Three and one-half times as many students enroll in French as
in German, 9 times more than in Spanish, 42 times more than in
Russian (*London Times,* 1978). In France and the Federal
Republic of Germany, the study of languages other than English
has diminished, although the European Economic Community
is giving higher priority to language learning: it may invest some

$8 million in 1980 in the teaching of nonnative European languages in order to increase student mobility and exchanges between the European countries.

Hopeful Signs

As in Europe, concern over the decrease in foreign-language study in the United States has led to efforts to seek out its causes and propose remedies. In December 1976, the MLA held a conference on "The Status and Future of Foreign-Language Study in the United States." Subsequently, the NEH funded "Task Forces for the Promotion and Development of Foreign-Language Study in the United States" for the period from September 1977 to June 1978. The five task forces dealt, respectively, with institutional language policy; the teaching of the commonly taught languages; training in the less commonly taught languages; public awareness; and government relations and national language policy. The final reports were completed in 1979, and the work of all five task forces is being integrated for the purposes of long-range follow-up. Most significant, the language-teaching profession, which encompasses a wide range of interests and educational viewpoints, is currently attempting to achieve a much-needed consensus on the priorities of foreign-language education.

The commitment of the United States and the 32 other signatory nations of the Helsinki accords of 1975 should provide further impetus to foreign-language teaching. One of the goals of the accords is "to encourage the study of foreign languages and civilizations as an important means of expanding communication among peoples for their better acquaintance with the culture of each country as well as for the strengthening of international cooperation." As mentioned earlier, one important result of this commitment has been the establishment of the President's Commission on Foreign Language and International Studies. One of the commission's major concerns is to evaluate the need for foreign-language proficiency on the part of college and secondary school students and, assuming that such a need exists, to discover and recommend the most effective methods of teaching foreign languages to American students. Foreign-language study must not be seen merely as "an ornament for the cultivated" (Starr, 1978a, p. 28); it must be viewed as an important asset for prospective employees of government, of businesses with international interests, and of many other sectors of society.[2] Employers must be persuaded to recognize proficiency in a foreign language as an asset and the lack of such proficiency as a handicap. Even the Foreign Service has not had a foreign-language entry requirement in recent years —having abandoned it partly because it seemed to favor graduates of certain institutions—although in order to be commissioned in the Foreign Service, one must gain proficiency in a "working" (as opposed to "dead") foreign language within two years after entering the service.

More important even than its relevance to specific jobs, mastery of a foreign language must be recognized as enhancing students' appreciation of their culture and of language per se— their own language and culture as well as the foreign one. Young people should recognize the importance of exposure to different cultures through study abroad, summer travel and work programs in other countries, the Peace Corps, inner-city programs, work on Indian reservations, and so forth—in short, wherever there is an opportunity to come into contact with a different language or culture group. If students seek out such opportunities, I believe that their institutions will be motivated to prepare them for these experiences by emphasizing the advantages of acquaintance with a second culture and proficiency in a second language. Teachers of foreign languages should stress the importance of culture and take literally the expression "a living language." Innovative and imaginative foreign-language teaching is already a reality, one example being the program initiated by John Rassias, Professor of Romance Languages at Dartmouth College (Luxemberg, 1978). Rassias's approach combines intensive on-campus immersion in a foreign language

[2]The publication *Options for the Teaching of Foreign Languages, Literatures, and Cultures* of the American Council on the Teaching of Foreign Languages points up the variety of careers for which foreign-language proficiency is important and gives information on language programs at colleges and universities oriented toward those careers (Born and Buck, 1978).

with a subsequent ten-week stay with a family in the country where that language is spoken.

In recent years, an incentive for foreign-language study has been provided by the increasing cultural and linguistic self-awareness of minority groups, which are placing greater emphasis on preserving their "roots" rather than being blended in the "melting pot." School children from families that speak a foreign language enroll in that language at a rate at least double that of children from English-speaking families. OE's Office of Bilingual Education supplies substantial funding for transitional programs in bilingual, bicultural education; such programs enable children whose first language is not English to pursue their education in their own language while also learning English. Among the languages for which such programs are available are Chinese, French, Italian, and Spanish (Spanish is spoken by the children in 80 percent of the federally funded programs). Foreign-language studies should benefit from this support of bilingual education, although current legislation does not authorize bilingual programs to teach foreign languages to English-speaking children.

A 1978 amendment to the 1975 Bilingual Education Act does provide for the participation in bilingual instruction of up to 40 percent of all children whose home language is English. In fact, however, a directive of the U.S. Department of Health, Education, and Welfare calls for an enrollment ratio of at least 75 percent for English-limited students in bilingual programs, and cultural teaching tends to be deemphasized.

It is not clear exactly how bilingual-education programs relate to foreign-language teaching in the United States. It is increasingly apparent, however, that some interrelationship does or can exist and that the presence in the United States of some 30 million people whose first language is not English should be seen as a resource for foreign-language learning. If current values in federal programs cause English-limited children to lose their foreign-language skills deliberately or unconsciously, this diminishes the nation's foreign-language resources and affirms the ambivalence of Americans toward foreign-language skills.

If students whose first language is English were encouraged

to become bilingual at the same time—even in the same classes—that the non-English-speaking students are acquiring English, this would greatly improve current bilingual programs by bringing the two groups of students together. Too often, such programs isolate one group from the other, a result that runs counter to the goal of genuine bilingualism. Bilingual programs should also incorporate exchanges among families, similar to those included in study-abroad programs, so that students from both the English-speaking and non-English-speaking groups can live—overnight, for meals, or for a period of a week or more—in a different cultural and linguistic milieu.

In this chapter, which focuses on language study and its place in a general-education curriculum, I want to emphasize that the basic aims of foreign-language study remain the same: proficiency in another language and familiarity with another culture as well as increased understanding and appreciation of one's own culture. Finally, a crucial element in strengthening foreign-language study in the United States is a major effort to make the American public aware that the United States can no longer afford to be monolingual. The foreign-language profession and the colleges and universities should work closely with industry and government—and with the President's Commission on Foreign Language and International Studies—to achieve this wider awareness. The advanced studies and the specialized training and competencies needed for international fields are discussed in a later chapter, as are study-abroad programs.

5

International Student Exchanges

Gardner, in writing about the kinds of leadership the world needs, calls for "shapers of what might be" and "renewers of the society." He emphasizes the importance of identifying such leaders when they are young and providing them with "the kind of experience that will strengthen them for the work they must do." "One could conceive of quite a variety of educational goals for such young people, but there is one fundamental that outranks all others: they must be exposed to experiences that broaden their horizons, lift them out of their specialties, introduce them to other worlds, other views, and the farflung variety of the modern world."[1]

What better way to accomplish this goal than through international student exchanges?

Foreign Students in the United States

The presence of an estimated 250,000 students from other countries at American colleges and universities offers a readily available way of introducing American students to "other worlds, other views." It also challenges colleges and universities to ensure that the foreign students they admit will be able to fulfill their academic goals. To American society at large, the

[1]J. W. Gardner letter to J. E. Slater (President, Aspen Institute for Humanistic Studies), March 23, 1978, pp. 5-6.

presence of foreign students (and other foreign visitors) requires a special effort because, in President Carter's words, "We want them to understand our values, our institutions—the vitality of our culture—and how these relate to their own experience" (International Communication Agency [ICA], 1978, p. 23).

Foreign-Student Enrollments

The number of foreign students in American colleges and universities has increased dramatically from 53,100 in 1960-61 to an estimated 250,000 in 1977-78. However, relative to the total number of students in higher education, they have remained below 2 percent since 1960. Although the United States enrolls more foreign students than any other developed nation, it ranks twenty-first in terms of the percentage of students coming from other countries. Among the countries with significant percentages of foreign students are Canada (16.9 percent), Switzerland (15.6 percent), France (12.4 percent), Austria (10.7 percent), and the Federal Republic of Germany (9 percent) (Julian and Slattery, 1978).[2] Thus, on a relative enrollment basis, the United States is not a leader among the nations that offer higher-education opportunities to foreign students.

If foreign students are to serve as a resource for internationalizing American education, it is important to know the kinds of institutions and programs in which they are enrolled, and at what level, as well as the countries they come from. The majority are undergraduates (53 percent in 1976-77) (Julian and Slattery, 1978), and the greatest recent increase has occurred in the community colleges: from 10 percent of all foreign students in 1970-71 to 15 percent in 1975-76 (College Entrance Examination Board, 1978b).[3] But the foreign-student population in the U.S. is clustered; close to half are at the major research universities.

---

[2]It should be emphasized that these figures are not wholly reliable, because they were based on college and university surveys for which returns, though high, were not 100 percent.

[3]These estimates include students on immigrant visas, a large number of whom are from Cuba.

Among the fields in which foreign students were enrolled in 1976-77 are engineering (24.1 percent), business and management (17 percent), the natural and life sciences (11.3 percent), social sciences (10.3 percent), humanities (7.1 percent), and agriculture (6 percent). The percentage of women in the foreign-student population has gone up from about one-fifth to close to one-third in the past 20 years (Julian and Slattery, 1978). Moreover, in recent years the number of foreign students whose children are also in the United States has increased so rapidly that the National Association for Foreign Student Affairs (NAFSA) has set up a special committee on foreign students in elementary and secondary schools.

The geographic origins of foreign students have changed significantly since the mid-1960s. The greatest change is the dramatic increase in students from OPEC countries—from 14,090 in 1971-72 to 52,040 in 1976-77, or close to one-fifth of all foreign students in the U.S.[4] The largest increases are shown in the following figures (Julian and Slattery, 1978):

	1971-72	*1976-77*
Iran	6,365	23,310
Kuwait	406	1,240
Nigeria	2,894	11,870
Saudi Arabia	821	4,590
Venezuela	1,703	5,750

These figures are probably low because of the difficulty of obtaining precise enrollment data. Some experts claim that there are over 50,000 Iranian students in the U.S. and that this figure will increase by 100 percent in the next five years. (Since the shah's ouster, this projection has been revised downward.) The number of Saudi Arabian students will also go up. According to Talal Hafiz of the Saudi Arabian Educational Mission, even with the $21 billion invested in education in his country in 1975-1980, fewer than half of those graduating from high

---

[4]Worldwide, OPEC-country students accounted for 25.6 percent of all foreign students in 1976-77 (Julian and Slattery, 1978).

school each year can be accommodated in Saudi Arabia's higher-education system, and the government intends to send more students to the United States because the flexibility of American higher education is well adapted to Saudi Arabian needs (Hafiz, 1978).

Another significant group of foreign students will be sent by the People's Republic of China (PRC), beginning with around 50 in late 1978 and reaching a figure of close to 500 in 1979 and possibly 1,000 to 2,000 by the early 1980s. This is part of a major PRC overseas-study program through which 10,000 to 20,000 students will study abroad in the next several years. The fact that the majority are likely to be scholars who have been sent abroad to reinforce their training, rather than undergraduates, will be an important element in the cultural adjustment process.

Foreign Students as a Resource

Other recent and predicted changes in the composition of the foreign-student population in the United States offer special problems and opportunities. The large number of students from the OPEC nations enrolled in U.S. colleges and universities provide an opportunity for American students—and faculty—to become acquainted at first hand with people from countries that directly affect the American economy and way of life. A greater effort is needed in this area—an effort that could build on past experience—because American colleges and universities have a long tradition of encouraging contact and interchange between foreign and American students and between foreign students and the wider community.

Since its founding in 1948, NAFSA has given increasing priority to programs that involve foreign students in the local community, especially through its Community Section, a professional group committed to enriching the informal educational experience of foreign students. Community activities typically include visits in the homes of American families (for example, for Thanksgiving dinner), foreign-student participation in civic groups, visits to places of cultural and historic interest, and the like. But foreign students also directly contribute to the international education of Americans through community programs. According to Hugh Jenkins, Executive Vice President of NAFSA (1978, p. 15), "True to the concept of interchange, many of these programs involve foreign students as active participants in cooperative ventures. Thus, while foreign students have been offered special opportunities to visit American Indian schools . . . and meet with groups of professionals in their particular field of study, they have also served as volunteers in community-action programs, shared in intercultural communications workshops, and been involved in programs at local high schools and community clubs."

In the past few years, a number of colleges and universities have made a more deliberate effort to use foreign students as an international-education resource in formal academic programs as well as informal activities. Foreign students help orient American students who are about to study in their countries; they tutor American students in their languages; and they advise and participate in cross-cultural workshops designed to analyze intercultural values and attitudes and to identify and eliminate cultural stereotyping.

The use of foreign students in formal learning programs offers a unique means to strengthen international education in a variety of disciplines and, incidentally, provides an added justification for the presence of foreign students at American colleges and universities. At the University of Minnesota, which has been particularly active in this field (with NAFSA support), foreign students add cross-cultural content to many courses through classroom teaching at the instructor's invitation. Another example of this approach at another university is a session in a course on gerontology in which students from India, Japan, and the People's Republic of China describe attitudes toward the elderly in their societies. At a number of institutions, foreign students serve as a learning resource by agreeing to be interviewed by American students who seek an international perspective for a particular assignment or project.

Foreign students can and should be urged to add an international dimension to existing courses. Although some foreign students, especially at the graduate level, cannot take the time to contribute in these ways, and despite the fact that such contributions must be carefully planned and must not impose on students' privacy, experience has shown that many foreign students welcome opportunities to become involved in this type of arrangement. They are more than willing to help Americans understand their home countries better. More two-way opportunities of this sort should be provided for both foreign and American students.

Problems and Needs

Essential to the success of cross-cultural programs like those described in this chapter are committed and professionally trained staff members to evaluate, advise, and follow up on foreign students. This is especially true in view of the growth in the foreign-student population and the increasing concentration of large numbers of students from a few countries at individual institutions—particularly the community colleges, where in some instances there may suddenly be 100 or 200 foreign students, mostly from a single country, enrolled in technical and paraprofessional programs of special relevance to their country. This situation can produce strains and tensions that can become serious when there is insufficient staff to handle foreign-student affairs. (The community colleges have, however, done much to improve their capacity to deal with foreign students. Beginning in 1977, and with the help of the central office of the American Association of Community and Junior Colleges [AACJC], they organized themselves to cope with the first wave of a major influx of Nigerian students.)

NAFSA makes a vital contribution to foreign student services and to programs designed to increase foreign students' knowledge of American life. In implementing the Mutual Educational and Cultural Exchange Act of 1961, the purpose of which is "to enable the government of the United States to increase mutual understanding between the people of the United States and the people of other countries," the Department of State has financed the NAFSA Field Service. This agency enhances the expertise of those involved in educational exchange programs through training grants, campus consultations, workshops, and publications.

NAFSA's Cooperative Projects Program, funded since

1967 by the Department of State, has supported over 58 projects aimed at enriching the educational experience of foreign students. Still another program, directed by a NAFSA-AID committee, supports research and projects involving AID-sponsored students. Although these programs account for a tiny fraction of the budgets of their sponsoring agencies, they represent over two-thirds of NAFSA's annual budget and enable it to strengthen and extend its valuable foreign-student services and programs.

For foreign students to be an asset to American colleges and universities, foreign-student admission and advisory services must be adequate to meet new demands and trends, even though the pressures of finance and declining enrollments may motivate some institutions to cut back on these services. However, declining enrollments have spurred some institutions and agencies to undertake active recruitment of foreign students for income purposes without paying sufficient attention to the students' educational qualifications or the institution's capacity to meet their academic needs. This situation is exacerbated by the fact that a number of countries permit their students to leave the country to enroll in an "English as a Second Language" program without having been admitted to a degree program at a U.S. college or university. Many such students end up at institutions that are indifferent to their needs. *Guidelines for the Recruitment of Foreign Students,* a publication (1978c) of the College Entrance Examination Board's Advisory Committee on International Education, is designed to help colleges and universities recruit foreign students more responsibly. An intensified effort is needed to prevent American institutions from exploiting foreign institutions—and vice versa.

Also pertinent to foreign students' academic needs is a joint study by NAFSA and the Council of Graduate Schools (1979a) on the extent to which American universities are willing to modify their requirements and enhance the relevance of their graduate programs to foreign students. This subject was one of several issues discussed at a conference held by the Institute of International Education (IIE) in February 1979. As American graduate-student enrollments decline and foreign students account for as much as 30 percent of enrollments in some graduate programs, it is important to determine whether the advanced training that foreign students receive in the United States is as relevant as possible to their careers.

Another factor affecting the contribution of foreign students to the education of American students is financial. As Francis X. Sutton of the Ford Foundation has observed, financial pressures are increasingly skewing foreign-student enrollments toward "the rich and the desperate." Rising tuition costs in private institutions and out-of-state tuition in public colleges and universities make study in the United States more and more difficult for foreign students who have neither rich parents nor a sponsoring agency. This trend is aggravated by the decrease in the funds available for tuition and other support by American institutions for foreign students, which were the primary source of funds for only 12.7 percent of foreign students in 1976-77 compared with 25 percent only a few years ago (U.S. General Accounting Office, 1976). Financing American education for foreign students is further hindered by the restrictions imposed by the Immigration Service on opportunities for foreign students to work while in the U.S., even during the period of practical training for which they are eligible after earning their degree and before going home. The upshot of these trends is that a substantial percentage of foreign students are from the most affluent sector of their society, and the American students who rub elbows with them may obtain a distorted view of their cultures.

Federal funding of the Fulbright scholarship program has provided support for close to 50,000 foreign students since the program began in 1949. However, the number of students supported annually dropped from around 1,800 between 1949 and 1968 to about half that number in the early 1970s, but has risen appreciably since then to 1,900 in 1978-79. The decrease in Fulbright scholarships has been relative, if not absolute, in that foreign-student enrollments in American colleges and universities have more than quadrupled since the inception of the program. This trend, in turn, supports the trend of most foreign students coming from affluent backgrounds.

An impediment to cross-cultural learning may develop as a consequence of the increasing number of foreign students who reflect considerable affluence with strong cultural differences. An extreme example is the Middle Eastern student in a private American cooperative secondary school who telephoned his father to send over a servant to do his daily dishwashing assignment! Special efforts are needed to bridge this kind of cultural gap.

Why Admit Foreign Students?

While the enrollment of foreign students in American colleges and universities can make a major contribution to international education, there are other important rationales for admitting foreign students to U.S. institutions. Some of these were enumerated at a seminar held in March of 1978 under the joint sponsorship of the Rockefeller Foundation and the IIE (Burn, 1978, p. 14).

> Exchanges enhance the balance-of-payments position of the country in which foreign students pursue their higher education both because they spend money in it while there and because they favor the country in commercial and other relationships in which they may be involved professionally on returning home. International student exchanges—especially those that involve advanced students—contribute to scholarship worldwide and to the emergence of international centers of excellence, since a condition of their excellence is their capacity to attract the best brains regardless of country of origin. Exchanges are important to international political and other relations, as they enable the potential political leadership —the exchange students—of a country to understand the circumstances and values of the country where they pursue their higher education, and how and why that country makes decisions. It was also agreed that student exchanges do not automatically assure greater international understanding; they must be carefully planned and administered or they may be more cosmetic than useful in bridging cultures.

In view of the rapid increase in foreign-student enrollments in American postsecondary education in the past few years, together with the negative reverberations following several episodes of foreign-student protest and conflict and the impact of irresponsible "hustling" for foreign students by some American colleges, it is more important than ever to ensure that foreign students are recruited in a responsible manner and that they are viewed as a positive resource for international education. A basic reason for encouraging students from other countries to pursue their studies in the United States is that many, if not most, of those students achieve positions of leadership in their home countries and constitute a network of intellectuals who are familiar with American life and values even though they may not support them. Hence, every effort should be made to make sure foreign students have a beneficial sojourn in the United States; that mismatches between students' educational goals and the institutions in which they enroll are avoided; and that the students gain a wide acquaintance with American life and values.

Responsibilities of Foreign Students

In view of the vigorous debate generated by recent episodes of foreign-student protest, some mention of the responsibilities of students outside their home country is in order here. According to NAFSA (1979b), these (unenforceable) responsibilities include the following:

1. Strive to understand and tolerate a host country's educational and cultural setting, including standards of conduct, law, respect for others, honesty, and integrity.
2. Respect rights of self-determination of others.
3. Observe the laws and respect the culture of the host country.
4. Participate as fully as possible in the life of the host university and country.
5. Seek to participate in joint and cooperative ventures of an educational, social, or cultural nature with citizens and students of the host country and with other international students and scholars.
6. Individually and in groups, act with respect for the rights of

persons from other countries, cultures and subcultures, without abridging those rights even in the pursuit of one's own rights.

7. In general, by actions and deeds, accept responsibility for the best interests of international educational interchange programs, so as to gain the largest amount of public support for them, and the widest possible involvement in them.

American Students Abroad

The fact that international educational exchanges build important ties between nations is illustrated by the introduction of the Ph.D. degree to British universities. Discussions of the desirability of the Ph.D. go back to the first congress of the universities of the British Empire in 1912, when the Ph.D. was resisted as a "Germanic novelty." The intervention of Lord Balfour, foreign secretary during World War I, tipped the balance in the debate and led to the adoption of the Ph.D. by the University of London in May 1918. After a mission to the United States to further Anglo-American cooperation, Balfour became convinced that Great Britain, not Germany, should be the European country to which American students were sent for foreign study.[5]

In 1973, the most recent year for which worldwide figures are available, 700,000 students were studying in countries other than their own, accounting for 2 percent of all enrollments in higher education. Students from the United States constituted the largest group, although they represented only 0.3 percent of American college and university students.

The following figures show the number of American students studying abroad in recent years:[6]

1962	12,500
1970	25,000
1973-74	33,500
1975	70,000
1977-78	120,000

[5]Information obtained from Guy Neave, the Institute of Education, Paris.

[6]The sources for these figures include the Institute of International Education (1977a), Perkins (1971), Academy for Educational Development (1975), and UNESCO (1975).

These figures tend to include only students in organized programs and exclude the increasing number who enroll directly in universities and colleges abroad or pursue independent study; thus, they are on the low side. Passport statistics suggest a continuing relatively steady increase, as shown in the following table:[7]

	Passports Issued to Students[a]
1951	23,970
1963	133,150
1973	558,950
1975	405,990
1976	478,090
1977	533,420
1978	596,660

[a]Students refers to those indicating they are students on their passport applications.

U.S. college-sponsored academic-year-abroad programs totaled 804 in 1979-80, and 904 summer programs were offered in 1979. Data on these programs, also incomplete, suggest not only steady growth but also greater diversity among the institutions involved. Whereas in 1965 few members of the American Association of State Colleges and Universities offered overseas-study programs, by 1975 over 30 percent of the 324 state colleges and universities offered such programs (Gray, 1977). A questionnaire sent to 640 community colleges by the Council on International Educational Exchange in 1977 showed that 50 of the 282 responding institutions offered overseas-study programs and that an equal number were interested in doing so in the future (CIEE, 1978). In 1978, the International/Intercultural Consortium of the American Association of Community and Junior Colleges (AACJC) reported 39 summer programs offered by 27 community colleges, plus 9 offered by Los Angeles community colleges and 46 by Rockland (New York)

[7]Information obtained from U.S. Passport Office.

Community College.[8] Although current figures on overseas programs for teacher education are not available, it seems likely that these have also increased since 1971. All of these programs are primarily at the undergraduate level.

Along with the greater variety of institutions offering study-abroad programs has come greater variety in the students who participate, in their fields of study, and in the countries in which they pursue their studies. Whereas in 1966-67 more than half of all American students abroad were in France, Mexico, and Canada, and slightly more than half were studying the humanities, the range of countries and disciplines has widened. However, according to William H. Allaway, Director of the University of California's Education Abroad Program, this trend may be reversing:[9] "Another current trend is away from the Third World. There is some interest (perhaps increasing) in Latin America, somewhat less interest in Africa, less interest in Asia by far than a few years ago, and relatively few students wanting to study in the Arab countries, although the interest in Israel is sustaining itself well. Perhaps part of the cooling of idealism, the trend toward security, and the desire to have an education that will provide job training is reflected in greater interest in the major language areas rather than the countries which require considerable background to cope with in any meaningful way."

Another trend related to study abroad is the increasing number of students who go abroad for independent study, to serve as interns, or to participate in practical training programs. The International Association for the Exchange of Students for Technical Experience (IAESTE) is an organization with member chapters in 44 countries that arranges international student exchanges for practical training programs. Through these exchanges, students—mainly but not exclusively in engineering and technology—gain two to three months of practical experience in industry. The organizations offering training pay the

[8]Information obtained from AACJC.

[9]William H. Allaway to Barbara B. Burn, Nov. 11, 1977.

students enough to cover their living costs. Since the IAESTE program began in 1948, it has sent 2,850 U.S. students abroad for temporary training.

At the graduate level, there has probably been a decline in overseas study and research as funding for them has diminished. Until the late 1950s, the number of postgraduate awards for American students administered by the IIE was around 1,000 annually (mainly Fulbright grants); in the early 1960s they dropped to 800 to 900 annually, and in 1968 they took a nosedive to approximately 350. Since then they have increased gradually; 500 awards will be offered in 50 countries in 1980-81. (The application rate has been around 3,000 per year.)[10]

Benefits of Study Abroad

The values of overseas study, both tangible and intangible, are compelling for those who have had this opportunity as well as for their parents, acquaintances, and teachers. The contribution of study abroad to personal growth and academic motivation and achievement is widely acknowledged. But as long as less than 1 percent of college and university students study abroad annually, the constituency will remain insufficient to stimulate significant institutional or national support for overseas study.

W. H. Auden (1937) provided one rationale for study abroad when he said that "no one can understand his own country unless he has lived in at least two others." Other rationales include giving students opportunities to develop linguistic skills, to experience and learn to understand another culture, to obtain a comparative view of their major field, and to gain knowledge and skills that will be useful in a career in government, business, teaching, and many other fields. Study abroad may also enhance qualifications for admission to graduate or professional study. Finally, undergraduate study abroad leads to higher enrollment in graduate programs in international relations, international trade, comparative studies, and foreign languages and area studies.

Beyond these values, the experience of living and studying

[10]Information obtained from IIE.

in another country is a way of bringing people from one country into closer communication with those in another. Often these are people who are likely to have important responsibilities and considerable influence in their own country. It is noteworthy that, since 1976, the European Economic Community has given high priority to international student exchanges. It now supports 80 joint-study programs operating between universities in two or more member states. If American institutions take the goal of strengthening international education seriously, overseas study should be significantly expanded as one of the more effective means to this end.

Problems

Although overseas study can be an immensely rewarding experience, it is not without problems. "Island" or "ghetto" programs —which transport American students abroad, use American faculty (sometimes selected for reasons other than suitability for overseas teaching) or "moonlighting" local teachers, and have the students living and studying with each other rather than with native students—do little to facilitate the direct contact with the foreign culture and society that is such an essential ingredient of study abroad. Other deterrents to overseas study are its rising cost, due to both inflation and the deterioration of the dollar; the decline in foreign-language study in the United States and the concomitant reduction in student motivation and capacity for overseas study; and restrictions on foreigners working abroad—indeed, the working scholar is a disappearing phenomenon in most countries. The increasing concern of some American institutions to fill their own classrooms and dormitories is another, more subtle, obstacle. Often this concern is expressed as doubts about the academic quality of study-abroad programs, even though study abroad typically raises the student retention rate (that is, the number who stay to complete their degrees increases, perhaps because study abroad typically strengthens students' motivation and academic goals).

The paucity of scholarship aid for undergraduate study abroad is another deterrent, although students at some institutions are able to use federal aid to study abroad. An exception is a program funded by the International Communication Agency (ICA), the goal of which is to encourage minority students to study abroad. Colleges and universities could help alleviate this problem by ensuring that students who are eligible for Basic Education Opportunity Grants can avail themselves of this aid when studying abroad. Work-Study funding should also be available for study abroad.

Another problem that deserves some attention is the relationship of overseas study to other programs and concerns of American universities and colleges. At many institutions, study abroad is not recognized as a legitimate academic experience meriting institutional financial support along with other academic programs. All too often, study-abroad programs are expected to be self-financing. Some colleges and universities even operate such programs as a source of revenue. Allaway describes this problem as follows:[11] "We continue to have operating in the field entrepreneurs, both with official academic anointment and without, who exploit resources overseas and exploit the interest of students who cannot get the guidance on their home campuses to aid them in distinguishing between sound programs and those that are run either ineptly or simply for profit. The most dangerous to the other programs are the American institutions which exploit their status as academic institutions in order to take advantage of the good will of institutions overseas and then do not back this with proper planning, supervision, and reciprocal activities, so that study abroad is viewed as a desirable phenomenon by those on the receiving end."

Undergraduate overseas study is often a low priority for American colleges and universities. Faculty members may regard it as peripheral to their interests unless it gives them a chance to go abroad. In many cases the administration of study-abroad programs is insufficiently integrated into curricular programs on campus. Study-abroad advisers may be perceived primarily as "people movers" and have relatively little clout with the administration and little communication with the faculty. Moreover, rarely are study-abroad and foreign-student affairs

[11]William H. Allaway to Barbara B. Burn, Nov. 11, 1977.

integrated so that they complement and reinforce each other, particularly when the American institution enrolls students from countries to which it sends its own students. What a waste it is to have students from a particular country on campus in complete isolation from students on the same campus who are preparing to study in that country!

The administration of overseas study may be deficient in several other respects. Advisers and their students may lack the knowledge to select among the vast number of available programs, although NAFSA and IIE are very helpful in this regard. As a result, many students go abroad inadequately prepared for the experience. Moreover, few college or universities have follow-up programs in which the student's overseas experience is reinforced and integrated into his or her ongoing activities so that it can have a "multiplier effect" on other students and on the intellectual climate of the institution. All of these problems call for more effective institutionalization of study abroad, a step that requires much more commitment on the part of senior administrators and faculty. Only with such commitment is overseas study likely to be given the staffing and funds that are essential for effective functioning.

Another problem area is the matter of accreditation: Regional accrediting associations do not evaluate overseas study programs. Ways should be found to hold American colleges and universities accountable for the quality of their overseas activities. The Council on International Educational Exchange (CIEE), a consortium of over 170 academic institutions and educational organizations, performs on-site evaluations of overseas programs, but, because this is confined to programs of member institutions and is done only on request, most study-abroad programs are not involved (CIEE, 1978). Quality control remains at the discretion of the institution operating the program.

Attempts to measure systematically the effects of overseas study on students are also fragmentary and insufficient. Antioch College recently carried out a survey of the impact of its program of study and work abroad on students who participated in the program during the 1960s. Although the response rate to its questionnaire was low, the findings confirmed the value of the experience. The percentage of students in the program who completed their degrees and went on to graduate study was higher than the figure for average students. More of those who study abroad continue to read books in a foreign language, keep up with current events, and spend time abroad (Abrams, 1978).[12]

Another recent study on the "Euro-consciousness" of American college students (Markovits and Keeler, 1978) showed that students who had been abroad for six or more months were significantly better informed about Western Europe and had more positive attitudes toward it than students who had not lived or studied in Europe, and that the extent and intensity of the experience made it more valuable to them. The survey concluded (p. 10): "Direct contact *does,* in general, make a significant positive difference in both knowledge and attitudes. On virtually every knowledge question, the 64 percent of the sample who had ventured across the Atlantic scored significantly higher than their peers who had not done so."

Still other evaluations have been carried out or are in progress, including studies on long-term effects of studying abroad and the coping skills needed to adapt to foreign environments (Hull, Lemke, and Ting-ku Houang, 1977). A 1976 study of the Eisenhower Exchange Fellowships—though focusing on mid-career professionals in government, industry, and education rather than on degree students—is relevant to the broad question of overseas experience; it is noteworthy that 74 percent or more of the Fellows found the program "very effective in advancing their understanding of the U.S. and its people . . . and in helping them interpret the U.S. to their countrymen" (Mark Associates, 1976, p. 8). Much more work is needed in this area. In fact, a study currently being conducted under UNESCO sponsorship by the University of Massachusetts, Amherst, in collaboration with higher-education institutions in several other countries seems likely to show that evaluating the impact of study in the United States on students from other countries is

[12]Antioch's programs are not typical because they include work as well as study abroad.

even more difficult than measuring the impact of study abroad on American students.

The Future for Americans Studying Abroad

Several current trends are affecting opportunities for study abroad and seem likely to do so to a greater extent in the future. As more and more American students enroll in colleges and universities on a part-time basis rather than full time and as the percentage of college students who are not in the traditional 18- to 22-year-old age group increases, the number of students who are able to study abroad will decrease proportionately. Study abroad must be full time, and the student must be able to arrange for a leave of absence from job and other commitments —something that is often difficult or impossible for older students. A second trend relates to the growing emphasis on skill development in higher education, which will diminish the cultural focus that has long been characteristic of overseas study and lead to the recruitment of more students from professional fields, such as business administration, law, public health, and engineering.

A long-term trend in international student exchanges is the shift from free mobility to organized mobility or, as James A. Perkins has put it, from a laissez-faire to a restricted to a planned system (1978, p. 6):

> First came the "free market or laissez-faire stage." It was gradually replaced as higher education expanded after World War II by an increasingly complex set of requirements and conditions for study overseas: the "restricted market." We have not fully entered the restricted market era because the guidance is imperfect, the purposes uncertain, the restrictions are full of loopholes, and institutional and national differences vary so considerably as to allow great freedom of choice. . . . Yet . . . we are already moving into a third stage: as restrictions, rules, conditions, and difficulties multiply, the "planned market" emerges as the natural way to relieve the individuɑl of having to deal himself with the complexities of stage two.

At least two factors are moving educational exchanges from free to organized mobility. One is the limits that have been placed on foreign-student admissions. The French government requires foreign students to be admitted to a French university before they can obtain a visa to study in France; in addition, they must demonstrate adequate financial resources and show certification of good health. In June 1977, the National Office of French Universities and Schools stated that international educational exchanges with the United States and the European Economic Community were costing French taxpayers about $5 million (IIE, 1977b). (Foreign students do not pay tuition at French universities, and there are few French students abroad because study in other countries does not count toward their degrees.) This statement illustrates the concerns that are becoming increasingly typical of industrialized countries that enroll large numbers of foreign students (IIE, 1977b). A similar calculation for Great Britain showed instructional costs for foreign students of over $200 million in 1977-1980. This is a major factor in the increase in tuition for overseas students from £250 in 1967 to £705 in 1978-79; tuition for students from the affluent nations now threatens to equal full instructional costs (an estimated £2,500 per year).[13]

Absolute limits on foreign-student enrollments in the United Kingdom, Germany, the Netherlands, Denmark, and Sweden are another recent development. The Canadian government planned to prohibit universities from offering teaching and research assistantships to foreign students unless the positions were first advertised in Canada. This plan was withdrawn but remains a real possibility for the future. Owing to the widening of access to higher education in the industrialized nations in the 1960s and 1970s, colleges and universities have had difficulty accommodating all qualified students and have become increasingly reluctant to subsidize the postsecondary education of students from other countries. Student mobility has caused the system to close up—that is, the increase in openings for foreign students has not kept pace with demand—as students who are unable to gain admission to their home institutions

---

[13]Information obtained from Department of Education and Science staff, 1978.

have sought admission abroad, putting new pressures on other educational systems. In this way, student mobility may have hastened its own demise. Ironically, international cultural agreements, which in principle aim at facilitating student exchanges, have imposed requirements that may make mobility more difficult between countries that have such agreements than between those that do not.

In an attempt to cope with this situation, some American colleges and universities are entering into agreements with foreign institutions for reciprocal exchange of students. This trend, while commendable, may make it even more difficult for the individual American student to be admitted independently at an institution abroad, thus further limiting free mobility. In the United Kingdom in particular, the openings allocated to so-called occasional students may increasingly be filled under programs that provide for some form of reciprocity, and the individual American student will not be able to compete with these programs. However, in the long run the trend toward reciprocity will not only lead to equitable exchanges but also provide more opportunities to study abroad for students attending institutions with reciprocal exchange agreements.

To carry this a step further, special support, financial and otherwise, is needed so that American colleges and universities will be encouraged to develop overseas-study programs that are firmly rooted in reciprocity. While reciprocity may consist mainly of exchanges of students, the cooperating institutions can also strengthen each other's libraries, offer faculty members opportunities for foreign travel and research, and so forth. Regardless of the form it takes, reciprocity should be an essential component of international exchanges. Because relatively few American institutions can or are willing to provide the travel budgets necessary to support direct contact with institutions overseas, federal funding should contribute to these costs—on a selective and competitive basis. This is particularly true where non-Western countries are concerned, because the travel costs involved are higher and interinstitutional relationships are often more difficult to establish.

In dealing with the decreased availability of opportunities

for study in other countries, the American higher-education system operates under handicaps not found in more centralized systems. Given the pluralism of the American system, no single agency or organization can represent American higher education in negotiations on such matters—except, of course, the Department of State and the ICA in the area of cultural and educational exchange agreements. If the interests of American institutions in international exchanges are to be articulated effectively, the various institutions and professional associations active in this field—primarily IIE, CIEE, and NAFSA—should act more vigorously to develop a national capacity to influence policymakers to support overseas study for American students.

6

International
Faculty Exchanges

Why should scholars and teachers in one country be given opportunities to teach and do research in another? Numerous arguments are offered in defense of faculty exchanges, but in the end their justification and definition turn on the question of the universality of knowledge. Before we consider the current status of faculty exchanges, we should give some attention to this basic theme.

Historical Background

The medieval university aspired to universality. The base of all knowledge was humanity, and therefore all learning was global in scope. Thanks to this conception, Byzantine scholars were welcomed at Bologna and Florence and learned men from all of Europe felt at home in Paris, Oxford, and Cambridge. While regional cultural distinctions inevitably left a mark on the early universities, those distinctions were not considered relevant to the production and distribution of knowledge.

The Reformation did much to break down the universality of knowledge by erecting religious barriers in the world of learning; increasingly, these barriers came to correspond to the territorial boundaries of the nation-state. Hence, by the time of the Treaty of Westphalia in 1648, the basic values of the world of learning had become far more subject to parochial or regional influences. To be sure, the rise of science in early modern

Europe represented a contrary tendency; but the cosmopolitan nature of scientific learning was made possible in good measure by its increasing estrangement from questions of value.

During the past century and a half, both the national and cosmopolitan aspects of the world of learning have been strengthened. On the one hand, an immense increase in individual learning has taken place in disciplines based on quantitative modes of analysis. On the other hand, there has been an equally dramatic increase in the amount of knowledge that is based on the perceptions of particular cultural entities, national groups, or ideological factions. Historians of science would be quick to point out that even the quantitative fields have been far more subject to parochial influence than I seem to acknowledge. Even so, however, the split between the relatively cosmopolitan world of science and the often more provincial realm of the humanities and social sciences is real. Indeed, this polarization is clearly reflected in faculty exchanges. While the contrast should not be overstated, there is a tendency for scholars in the mathematically based fields to deal with one another as participants in a single transnational enterprise, while scholars in value-related fields often treat one another as representatives of the nation-state in which they live. Thus, international scholarly life reflects the degree to which we are willing to acknowledge the universality and unity of knowledge.

To what extent have these considerations affected the exchanges in which American scholars participate? It is worth noting at the outset that the United States has always welcomed foreign scholars and cultural figures, whose impact on American life has been immeasurable. When Mozart's librettist, Lorenzo Da Ponte, came to the New World, he was encouraged to establish the first program in Italian studies at what is now Columbia University. Even earlier, James Witherspoon, a Scot, was teaching James Madison the fundamentals of constitutional law at Princeton. Later, the post-1848 wave of German scholars helped link Americans with European scholarship, just as their successors in the 1930s were encouraged to share their knowledge with American students and colleagues.

Of course, these are examples of foreign scholars coming

to America rather than two-way exchanges. We were, in fact, rather slow to avail ourselves of the possibility of studying at foreign universities. Ralph Waldo Emerson's essay on "The American Scholar" (1839) did not promote such study, despite the fact that the essay itself was influenced by German thought. A few Americans did go abroad to study, some as artists, others as preachers or priests, and still others—especially in the later nineteenth century—as medical doctors. However, one gets the impression that this activity was considered to be far more appropriate for students than for faculty members. Of the younger Americans who went to Göttingen as students in the early nineteenth century, few, if any, ever went again as research scholars or guest professors.

With the benefit of hindsight, it is easy to assume that America's institutions of higher education played a major role in its intellectual contacts with the rest of the world. In fact, however, their role was modest at best. Scholars who came from abroad in the early days rarely went to American colleges, preferring to make contact with such organizations as the Smithsonian Institution and the American Philosophical Society. Even today, a formidable percentage of the intellectual contact between Americans and scholars from abroad occurs outside the university framework. To cite just two examples, the Western Electric Company maintains what amounts to an international graduate school, and the Department of Defense's National War University and affiliated institutions are also deeply engaged in teaching and research by individuals from several countries.

Faculty Exchanges in the Twentieth Century

Notwithstanding the extent of contact between American scholars and foreign institutions before World War I, there were few institutionalized programs of reciprocal exchange until after World War II, when both private and public institutions entered the field of two-way exchange. The Ford Foundation contributed richly to such programs, but at the core of two-way exchanges was the Fulbright program, which was created with funds made available through the renegotiation of outstanding European debts to the United States. There were at least three motives for the creation of the Fulbright exchanges. With regard to teaching, the principal motive was to foster intellectual contact between the United States and its wartime enemies as well as its allies. With regard to research, two further motives were present. On the one hand, the postwar years witnessed the emergence of large-scale fundamental research on American campuses. The enormous expansion in research budgets both reinforced and reflected a climate in which American scholars were inclined to frame ambitious research programs that included study abroad. On the other hand, precisely because of America's new emphasis on fundamental research, the United States became more attractive to foreign faculty members as a place to spend a semester or a year.

The relationship between teaching and research in faculty exchanges bears closer attention. Two-thirds of the American faculty members abroad on Fulbrights are engaged in lecturing rather than research. However, data gathered by Richard Lambert (1973) on scholars abroad under a variety of auspices show that research visits outnumber lecture tours by 3 to 1 in Mexico, 4 to 1 in the U.S.S.R., 5 to 2 in Iran, and so on. Lambert's data involve non-Western countries and other programs besides Fulbright; with regard specifically to Fulbright-sponsored foreign professors, far more conduct research than lecture at American institutions. As a consequence of the teaching/research imbalance in the Fulbright program, it is far more likely that a student at a major institution abroad will hear an American lecturer than that an American student will hear a foreign lecturer.

This imbalance may be attributed in good measure to language problems. The overwhelming majority of Americans who lecture abroad do so in English. This is certainly appropriate in English-speaking countries or in countries where second-language competence in English is a reality and not merely an official aspiration. It is less appropriate in the many countries where there is less knowledge of English. Even to foreigners who have mastered English, the visiting American who does not know the local language often appears as a kind of cultural imperialist. Such relations are rarely articulated, but they should not be ignored.

It is important to review the way international faculty exchanges are organized. Today, in contrast to former years, such exchanges are characterized by enormous diversity—a diversity that is far greater, in fact, than most reviews acknowledge. At least five types of programs exist. First, there are national programs funded by government sources, of which the best-known example is the Fulbright program. Second, there are programs that are national in scope but are funded in whole or in part by private sources. For example, until recently, the International Research and Exchange Board (IREX) was funded largely by nongovernmental sources. Third are programs involving links between specific university systems or groups of schools in this country and institutions or groups of institutions abroad. Ernest L. Boyer, former U.S. Commissioner of Education, did much to establish such an exchange between the State University of New York (SUNY) and Moscow University. Such programs remind us that a substantial part of the cost of international faculty exchanges is borne by state university systems and private institutions through sabbatical support. Fourth, there are numerous direct exchanges between U.S. campuses and schools abroad and even between individual departments within universities. Finally, there are faculty exchanges organized around specific projects that involve scholars from two or more countries. Professional organizations and associations often organize such exchanges, sometimes through governmental agreements. For example, the bilateral exchanges with the U.S.S.R. created in 1972 have moved large numbers of academic specialists and other experts between the U.S.S.R. and the U.S.A.

In all of these programs, the role of public funds has increased steadily, if only by default, while the private contribution has decreased proportionately. In this sense there appears to be a steady movement toward nationalization of scholarly contacts. But, while the importance of this growing dependence on public funds can scarcely be overestimated, it should not be seen as denying a role to private institutions. Indeed, the more formalized and centralized exchange programs become, the greater becomes the need for local entrepreneurs at the campus level. Rare is the successful exchange that does not depend on such people. Their importance is far greater than is revealed by the organizational charts of exchange agencies.

Current Problems

In our pluralistic system, it is difficult to obtain authoritative data on all the faculty exchanges that exist today. Clearly, however, those exchanges have a record of impressive achievement that should not be overlooked in focusing on their anomalies and problems.

Of the basic issues facing faculty exchanges, financial problems are by far the most pressing. Even though international faculty exchanges, like all other exchanges, are actually very inexpensive, they have become nearly impossible to fund adequately. At the local level, public funds for all forms of education are threatened by initiatives such as California's Proposition 13. At the national and international levels, the declining value of the dollar abroad has caused stipends for Fulbright Fellows to plummet in real value. Even though the senior Fulbright exchanges have had fairly constant funding over the past 10 years, the devaluation of the dollar has shrunk the real value of their budget by approximately one-half.[1] The junior exchange program has suffered even more, and the programs of the International Research and Exchange Board (IREX) and other agencies have experienced similar hardships.

The effects of this shrinkage in support would have been far less severe had it not coincided with a rapid expansion in the number of participating nations. When the Fulbright program was created, it focused on a handful of countries, largely in Western Europe. Today it has direct links with over 120 nations. Even within Western Europe, the number of institutions that would like to participate in such exchanges has increased dramatically. The 500 to 550 Americans who go abroad on Fulbrights each year therefore are spread out much more thinly than they once were. Although the number of exchanges has remained fairly constant, the intensity of American faculty contacts abroad has diminished in many important areas.

An impressive means of reducing financial problems has been to fund the Fulbright program on a more truly bilateral basis (although there are more than twice as many foreign Ful-

---

[1] Recent figures show a decrease of 59 percent (in constant dollars) in Fulbright funding since 1967.

bright recipients coming to the United States as there are American recipients going abroad, a situation that should be reviewed if educational exchanges are to reflect the greater reciprocity and mutuality that are supposed to characterize U.S. relations with other countries). Today the Federal Republic of Germany pays for 80 percent of its Fulbright exchange with the U.S., while France and Japan pay for 50 percent of their exchanges with the U.S. Much has been done to stretch the available funds; yet stipends for practically all American scholars abroad are now so low as to impose genuine hardship on many participants unless they secure supplementary funding, with the result that many distinguished faculty do not even bother to apply. Similarly, the relatively low stipends offered by most exchange programs discourage many senior foreign scholars and teachers from coming to the United States. Perhaps the time has come for funding to be shared equally by the United States and other nations, at least those in the developed world.

Another problem for faculty exchanges is the imbalance within the various exchanges. There are at least five types of asymmetry that bear mentioning. First, there is a persisting asymmetry in the types of American institutions hosting foreign scholars and teachers. Although a significant number of students coming from abroad attend less well-known American institutions, this is not yet the case with senior scholars, who go to the institutions that are best known abroad, largely on the basis of research done there 10 to 20 years ago. The result is a far greater concentration of visiting scholars at a small number of "research universities" than is probably healthy, because genuine research is taking place on hundreds of campuses today. The same conditions prevail for American scholars going abroad. It is easy to find an American scholar who will go to Paris, but harder to find one who is prepared to go to Toulouse. The result is a kind of funneling, which provides massive exposure to American teacher-scholars at a few major institutions, where exposure is scarcely needed, and no contact at all at the many institutions where such contact is most likely to be appreciated.

A second asymmetry exists among the types of American

institutions that send scholars abroad. While 71 percent of the faculty at major research institutions travel abroad at some point in their career, only 29 percent of junior-college faculty do. Obviously, some differential is to be expected, but one must ask how much is desirable. In 1975, the Board of Foreign Scholarships (BFS) recommended that second-, third-, and fourth-tier institutions participate more actively in exchange activity. This was a good recommendation, because many of the best young scholars are affiliated at those institutions, both in this country and abroad, for the simple reason that positions at the "major" institutions have been filled up through tenure.

A third asymmetry exists among American faculty members participating in exchanges. Lambert (1973) found that 79 percent of American international studies faculty never travel abroad for professional reasons, and another 7 percent have traveled only once during their career. The high degree of repeat participation by a minority of teachers and scholars has positive aspects, of course. (But the activities of that minority leaves no doubt as to the existence of an academic jet set.)

To some degree, this asymmetry reflects differences among academic disciplines. International scholarly and pedagogical exchanges are dominated by the fields of medicine and engineering. In 1967, for example, fully 64 percent of American exchange participants were from these two fields plus the natural sciences, and doctors and engineers travel abroad twice as much as scholars in the field of education. While the humanities almost approach the level achieved by engineering, the social sciences are far below them on the list, much closer to education.

What does this mean? Very simply, the more directly a field touches on questions of value as opposed to quantity, the more it is removed from international scholarly contact. To a striking extent, the increase in faculty exchanges reflects the "two cultures" of quantitative and qualitative learning mentioned earlier. One can certainly understand the relevance of American engineering to the developing world, but is it not regrettable that the social sciences are so parochial in their experience?

A fourth asymmetry involves the dramatic differences in

the degree of contact with specific foreign countries. The United Kingdom, France, Canada, and Germany claim fully three-fifths of all visits by American scholars abroad. Brazil, in contrast, accounts for only 2 percent of the total. India, too, is host to only 2 percent of American scholarly visitors of all types, but this figure is five times greater than the combined total for Pakistan and Afghanistan. Japan is also very low on the list, but it is visited 10 times more frequently than Korea. The U.S.S.R. accounts for only 4 percent of scholarly visits abroad. Clearly these differing levels of contact do not represent the intrinsic academic or political importance of the various countries to the United States.

The fifth asymmetry involves organization. The various international faculty exchanges are handled in this country by a group of highly professional, dedicated, and competent people. Thanks to their largely unheralded efforts, contact has been established and maintained with thousands of institutions and individuals abroad. In most cases such contact simply would not have existed without specialized American entrepreneurship. But given the centralized and/or authoritarian control prevailing in many foreign countries, American institutions are placed under pressure to operate in a more centralized fashion than they otherwise would. Paradoxically, such centralization, so important for the establishment of contact, takes a heavy toll in terms of local support. As a result, U.S. exchange organizations lack the strong, localized constituencies that are essential to their existence over the long term.

Possible Solutions

The problems just described call for action, and the following concrete proposals, long advanced by others, are action oriented.

1. The Fulbright program should be revitalized and funded to a degree that will enable it to meet its responsibilities and attract the best potential participants. Other major exchanges, including those with the U.S.S.R., Eastern Europe, and the People's Republic of China, should be placed on a secure

footing by the provision of federal and other support on a long-term basis.

2. The Board of Foreign Scholarships and other agencies concerned with scholarly exchanges should review the allocation of exchange resources and establish priorities by location and discipline. In this process, the relevant agencies should consult widely with scholars and other interested parties. But they must acknowledge that a very imperfect market system has permitted exchanges to be dominated by disciplines and professions in which there is a high degree of communication, often to the neglect of other locations and fields of study that are equally important.

3. All publicly sponsored exchanges, and private ones as well, should insist on a high degree of reciprocity. Nothing does more to sustain an exchange than the conviction on each side that it is obtaining great benefits from it; nothing does more to erode international scholarly contact than the suspicion of asymmetry in this regard.

4. With respect to organization, the administrators of the Fulbright program and other major exchanges should make a greater effort to foster direct, unmediated contact between individual scholars and institutions. They should also exploit every opportunity to root their programs more firmly at the state level in accordance with the federal structure of the American system.

5. The major programs, including the Fulbright program, should permit joint applications by scholars in two or more countries. This would foster both collaborative research and collaborative teaching.

During the past generation, a massive and successful effort has been made to open American higher education to contacts with scholars and institutions abroad. Now that the structure for such contacts is in place, it is possible to give thought once more to basic purposes. In spite of nationalistic pressures in various countries, the purpose of such exchanges is to foster learning in a wide range of disciplines that is global rather than national or parochial in scope. In the process of reexamining our scholarly contacts, it would be well to keep in mind this fundamental principle. For in the long run, teaching and research cannot be permitted to be captives of the nation-state.

Faculty Exchanges Today

To complete this review of international faculty exchanges and sojourns abroad, the remainder of this chapter will present the current state of the art of faculty exchanges, some of the objectives of such exchanges, the obstacles they face, the need to give them greater priority, and the difficulty of evaluating their contributions.

A reliable quantitative statement of the number of American academics who spend time abroad in a given year is impossible. Ten years ago this figure was estimated at 6,500, or only 1 percent of all college and university faculty. The Fulbright program now annually sends abroad about .001 percent of all college faculty, or 10 percent of those who go abroad each year. In 1977-78, this involved 530 lecturers and research scholars (Board of Foreign Scholarships, [BFS], 1977). Thus, while the Fulbright program is a prestigious one, it supports only a fraction of all international faculty exchanges. If, in the course of a 40-year career, every American faculty member were able to spend one semester abroad every 10 years, this would require a fivefold increase in the number of faculty going each year and a quadrupling of the number doing so under the Fulbright program.

Only a small percentage of American colleges and universities are involved in international exchanges, and the most active are the large research universities. It is not surprising that a 1977-78 survey on the involvement of university faculty in the developing countries showed that faculty from the larger institutions outnumbered those from the smaller ones by 4 to 1 (Atelsek and Gomberg, 1978). Even though state, teacher, and community colleges have more faculty going abroad for teaching or research now than they did a decade ago, fewer than one-fifth of these institutions participate in such activity.

Objectives

One of the major objectives of international faculty exchanges, which was stressed by George Kahn-Ackermann, Secretary-

General of the 22-member Council of Europe, is to meet the unprecedented need for national decision makers with an international frame of reference. Frank Thistlethwaite (1978), Vice-Chancellor of the University of East Anglia, stresses other objectives: collaborating in research, experiencing a different cultural and social environment, improving international relations by encouraging cross-fertilization between different cultures and ideas, and enhancing the role of universities as international institutions.

Obstacles

The obstacles to international faculty exchanges are imposing and real. The most concrete obstacle, of course, is finance. As we have seen, a sojourn abroad can be costly both to the individual and to the college or university involved. Federal funding supports only part of the cost of international educational exchanges. In 1968-69, for example, private support for exchanges of students, teachers, and scholars was calculated at $9.1 million, and public funding came to $11.6 million (BFS, 1969).

Support of exchange programs by other countries should also be noted. Of the 44 countries that have binational commissions to supervise their educational exchanges with the United States, over 20 invested a combined total of $4 million in these exchanges in 1976-77 (the U.S. contribution to exchanges with those countries was $5 million). This testifies to the commitment of other countries to such exchanges and makes possible a more substantial program than would be the case if the United States were the sole funding source (BFS, 1977). It should also be noted, however, that the existence of these binational commissions, some of which are not funded by the host country, contributes to the high overhead costs of Fulbright exchanges, thus significantly diminishing the funds available for program purposes.

The increase in governmental control is another obstacle to educational exchanges. Many countries, including the United States, are making it more difficult for foreigners to hold jobs, and such protectionism has a significant international effect on faculty mobility. This situation is exemplified by the restrictions on faculty recruitment in Ontario, Canada, which are based on the "head-and-shoulders" principle, whereby non-Canadians can be offered academic positions only if they are "head and shoulders" better than Canadian candidates.

The academic reward system also militates against international faculty exchanges. Institutions may regard sojourns abroad as a career interruption rather than enhancement, and the professional growth that can result from such sojourns may be overlooked at promotion time because it does not meet conventional criteria. As a result, untenured faculty are understandably reluctant to spend time abroad and often are given little encouragement to do so.

The increased responsiveness of higher education to local and vocational needs may also discourage faculty exchanges. The notion that universities are based in a particular community and should serve the interests of that community can produce a leadership that is more committed to the institution's local responsibilities than to its international involvements. International education could become a casualty of this tendency (Derham, 1978). In India, this trend is carried to an extreme; preference is given to in-state recruitment in faculty hiring (Murthy, 1978).

Another deterrent to American participation in international faculty exchanges is the tax situation abroad. As of 1979, France requires tax payments based on income earned from all sources, not just those located in France. More important, Americans living abroad seem likely to lose their $20,000 tax exemption; legislation passed in October 1978 reduces this amount to $15,000. The legislation does authorize a variety of deductions based on the higher cost of living overseas, with extra deductions for those living in so-called hardship areas. However, along with the slump in the dollar and rising costs abroad, the new legislation is likely to reduce the number of American scholars who are willing to take overseas assignments.

Priority Needs

It is regrettable that international faculty exchanges seem to be running into more obstacles than ever at a time when they should be given more priority than ever. As a consequence of the reduced growth rate of enrollments in American colleges, faculty hiring has been curtailed and the percentage of tenured faculty is rising. International faculty exchanges carried out on a one-to-one basis with institutions in other countries offer opportunities to diversify faculty at the home campus both by bringing in foreign visitors and by giving American faculty some experience in another environment. Excluding international travel costs, which now are relatively low between the United States and Western Europe, funds are needed only to "top off" salaries so that, regardless of discrepancies in the current value of the respective monetary units, visiting scholars are paid at levels appropriate to their professional experience and qualifications.

A one-to-one exchange obviously is much less expensive than simply inviting a foreign professor to teach at a U.S. institution. If they are carried out with the same foreign universities over several years, these international exchanges develop a continuity that not only makes for improved matching of academic needs and interests but also complements student exchanges between the participating institutions. Fulbright travel grants facilitate such exchanges by reducing the costs to the individual participants.

Evaluating Faculty Exchanges

The impact of faculty exchanges is difficult to evaluate because of the problem of selecting criteria for such an evaluation. To measure their impact solely in terms of the scholarly research and publications produced by professors who have gone abroad is to emphasize only one element among many. Much of the contribution of faculty exchanges cannot be quantified. Studies in West Germany, for example, have shown that German faculty return home from an academic year in the United States more aware of what it is to be "European." At the first national meeting of the American Fulbright Alumni Association, the intangible aspects of the Fulbright experience seemed especially important to the association's 1,500 members, as did the benefit to students, aptly expressed in the comment of a German professor that "knowledge needs distance."

As part of a comprehensive review of the U.S. government's exchange-of-persons programs, the General Accounting Office is examining the evaluation process in order to determine how to make it more effective. It will explore "the reception, assistance to, and follow-up provided for both foreign and American exchangees," including both student and faculty/research scholar exchanges (U.S. GAO, 1977b). The results of these surveys are not yet available, but, if they are as comprehensive as the planning suggests, they should help guide future policy formulation and administration in this area. With respect to the Fulbright Scholar Program, the lack of systematic records mentioned by Winks (1977) will make the GAO studies difficult to implement.

Any evaluation of educational exchanges should address itself to the criteria followed in publicly funded exchange programs. As pointed out earlier, the geographic distribution of Fulbright awards has long favored Western Europe and Canada, with one-third of the university lectureships and about 60 percent of the research awards allocated to those countries since 1949 (BFS, 1977). It is time to reassess the geographic allocation of these awards and to adapt it to the priorities of modern scholarship, national interest, and the world as it is today and will be tomorrow.

The administration of the Fulbright program might also be assessed. Attention should be given to the predeparture orientation of scholars, foreign-language needs and expectations (few Americans are able to teach in the language of the host country), and the contribution to faculty exchange of the relatively little-known OE-administered Fulbright program, which sponsored 698 scholars abroad between 1964 and 1976 (BFS, 1977). In short, if the experience of teaching, consulting, and doing research abroad is important to international scholarship, a careful look at faculty exchanges seems desirable, especially for the agencies that are most directly involved.

The International Communication Agency (ICA), as a first step toward carrying out its new responsibility for interagency coordination of international educational, cultural, and other programs conducted by the U.S. government (U.S. GAO,

1977b), is surveying all of the government's educational-exchange programs. An inventory of those programs is expected by late 1979, at which time ICA may pursue its coordinating role more actively. Meanwhile, the Fulbright Alumni Association, in cooperation with the President's Commission on Foreign Language and International Studies, has embarked on a major survey of the Fulbright experience. Undoubtedly, this survey and evaluation will also have its limitations. However, it is hoped that it will identify and document several important aspects of the Fulbright program, namely, its contribution to grantees' professional careers, their foreign-language proficiency and retention (and that of their families), and their knowledge of and concern about international issues.

7

The Role of American Universities in Development Assistance

Historical Background

While the United States has a long tradition of assistance to other nations, only since World War II have American universities served as a major resource in this area. Beginning in the 1950s, they entered into development assistance contracts with the Foreign Operations Administration, the International Cooperation Administration and, since 1961, the Agency for International Development (AID). The report of the Committee on the University and World Affairs (generally known as the Morrill Committee), published in 1960, asserted that American universities can play a major role in world affairs, a role that includes technical assistance in the developing nations.

In 1973, departing from its cold-war emphasis on higher education and economic infrastructure, American technical assistance took some new directions. The AID policy launched in that year called for concentration on "the poorest of the poor," that is, the 40 or 50 countries with annual per-capita incomes under $150 in 1969 dollars ($250-300 in 1976 dollars).

The new policy reflected disenchantment with AID's earlier emphasis on major projects such as building dams and roads and the failure of technical assistance to improve the living conditions of the poor majorities in less developed countries (LDCs).

Since 1975, there has been growing recognition that there are major differences among the LDCs. It is important to differentiate between the low- and middle-income countries—those with per capita incomes below U.S. $250 (based on 1976 GNP) and those with per-capita incomes above that level. Of the 770 million people living in absolute poverty in the developing world in 1975, 630 million were in the low-income countries and 140 million in the middle-income ones (World Bank, 1978). As a result of the improvement in conditions in the developing world, many LDCs, especially the middle-income countries, now need less infrastructural support and more scientific and technological development. The assistance they need is not so much unilateral aid as a collaborative relationship. American universities can play an expanded role in this new mode of development assistance if they have the commitment and resources to do so.

Along these lines, Title XII of the Foreign Assistance Act of 1975 is aimed toward a collaborative relationship between American agricultural colleges and universities and the LDCs in solving the world's agricultural and hunger problems. Its goals are to "strengthen the capacities of the United States land-grant and other eligible universities in program-related agricultural institutional development and research . . . improve their participation in the United States Government's international efforts to apply more effective agricultural sciences to the goal of increasing world food production, and in general . . . provide increased and longer-term support to the application of science to solving food and nutrition problems of the developing countries."[1] President Carter's proposal for an Institute for Scientific and Technological Cooperation (ISTC) provides for U.S. collaboration with the LDCs in science and technology.

[1] Public Law 94-161, 89 *Stat.* 861, December 20, 1975.

Agricultural Development

Title XII called for the establishment of a Board for International Food and Agricultural Development (BIFAD), partly because AID could not follow through on its promises and partly to involve U.S. institutions more actively in development assistance. BIFAD, which has seven members (four of whom are from universities), is an advisory body reporting to the administrator of AID. In general, it is involved in planning and programing AID's food and nutrition program, which accounts for some 55 percent of AID's budget. Its emphasis is on research, training, and extension services, as well as advisory services to the LDC ministries concerned with agriculture and nutrition.

BIFAD has several specific tasks, including identifying agricultural-development resources and needs in 16 LDCs (as of April 1978); supporting collaborative research in American universities and other institutions on agricultural-related problems that are of mutual interest to the United States and LDCs (for example, fisheries, aquaculture, and human nutrition); and providing so-called strengthening grants to eligible universities in the United States (if Congress agrees to fund such grants). The strengthening program will provide matching funds of up to $100,000 per institution plus a variable amount depending on how much Title XII activity the institution undertakes. To qualify for the funding, an institution must demonstrate its own financial investment in international agricultural programs.

BIFAD's collaborative research program is unusual in that it includes not only American institutions but also LDC universities and other agencies such as International Agricultural Research Centers. Moreover, its grants, which are broad in scope but largely commodity oriented, are for up to five years. In 1978, BIFAD approved a list of 20 priorities for such grants, and by 1979 two research projects were under way: one on small ruminants, with 13 participating universities, and another on sorghum and pearl millet. Other research projects were approaching the grant stage, and still others were in the proposal stage.

The BIFAD program offers American universities an opportunity for expanded participation in international agricultural research and is based on the expectation that they will become committed to such research. The proposed grants require even more explicit commitments. The purpose of the grants is to strengthen the university's capabilities in teaching, research, and extension work so that it can help LDCs build and strengthen their institutional research capacity and human resource skills, engage in collaborative research on food production and related matters, and become more equal participants in the international agricultural science network.

One of BIFAD's tasks has been to determine which U.S. universities are eligible to participate in the Title XII program. The legislation specified that land-grant and sea-grant institutions are eligible. Also eligible are institutions that are judged by BIFAD to have "demonstrable capacity and experience in the combined areas of teaching, research, and extension related to food and nutrition programs" (BIFAD, 1977, p. 3). By the end of 1977, BIFAD had built up a roster of 68 eligible universities, and others have been added since then.

In addition to requiring an expanded commitment on the part of the universities involved in its program, BIFAD enables them to participate more fully in the planning of AID's agricultural assistance by advising AID regarding its priorities and projects both in Washington and in the field. However, recent experience suggests that the agricultural universities may not have the capacity to handle an increasing number of AID projects; younger faculty are reluctant to take an assignment abroad lest they lose out on tenure; older faculty, many of whom had extensive experience abroad a decade ago, are less interested in such opportunities. A special problem is the matter of language proficiency, given the focus on the poorest countries. Many of those countries are French speaking, so agricultural faculty going there need—but rarely have—proficiency in French. To meet this need, AID contracts should fund intensive training in French for such faculty.

A further deterrent to the involvement of U.S. faculty in development assistance is the political instability prevailing in a number of developing countries. In addition, the sheer effort required to develop a Title XII proposal, especially in a period when enrollment and other pressures on agricultural colleges have intensified, militates against participation in the BIFAD program. Finally, although in some states eligible universities may be successful in obtaining additional state funds that qualify them for strengthening grants, in others the outlook for such funding is unfavorable.

Whether Congress will agree to fund BIFAD strengthening grants is uncertain. (By May 1979, BIFAD had recommended strengthening grants for 31 universities and was requesting $5 million for fiscal year 1979 and $9 million for fiscal year 1980.) Congress is somewhat suspicious of university research; some members believe federal funding of such research permits researchers to pursue personal interests, with little benefit accruing to the LDCs. They also wonder whether it duplicates the work of the International Agricultural Research Centers; if so, they favor increasing support for those centers rather than providing more funds for university research.

The relationship between AID and BIFAD, while it is better now than it has been in the past, is another problem area. AID remains suspicious of the universities and the validity of their contribution to the development process. While AID and BIFAD have agreed that BIFAD should participate actively in policy, strategy, budget, and program development, the way this will actually work is still evolving. In a paper presented to former AID Administrator Gilligan on August 18, 1978, Clifton Wharton, Chairman of BIFAD, noted that "the Agency still appears to have some difficulty in viewing Title XII in the fullest dimensions of its potential and accepting it as an integral part of the U.S. development assistance program in the food and nutrition area" (p. h). He referred specifically to the cool response of AID missions to Title XII and to the "continuation of the tradition that universities are 'hired' to do tasks as defined by the Agency and host country."

Development of Technology and Personnel

The contemplated reorganization of AID further complicates the BIFAD-AID relationship. The so-called Humphrey-Zablocki

Bill, initiated in 1977 and presented to Congress in 1978, proposes the first major restructuring of American foreign aid since 1961. Because the Senate Foreign Relations Committee's protracted Panama Canal debate prevented it from doing a careful study of the Humphrey Bill, consideration of the bill was postponed until 1979, when the committee planned to take a hard look at U.S. foreign-assistance policy and the machinery for implementing it.

The Humphrey-Zablocki reorganization plan drew on the Brookings Institution study, *An Assessment of Development Assistance Strategies,* commissioned by Secretary of State Vance in 1977. It emphasized the need to introduce new technologies, develop institutions, and train people, and recommended the establishment of a foundation to encourage effective development and use of science and technology in the LDCs. The Humphrey-Zablocki bill would replace AID with a new agency, the International Development Cooperation Administration (IDCA). A 1978 AID proposal outlines how it would pull together into a single organization AID, the Peace Corps, the Overseas Private Investment Corporation, the proposed Institute for Scientific and Technological Cooperation (ISTC), and a proposed multilateral development agency. IDCA would supersede AID and, either through the Secretary of State or directly at the cabinet level, have primary responsibility for coordinating the U.S. government's international-development activities.

The ISTC would represent a major change in U.S. international-development structures. It is conceived of as a semi-autonomous unit in IDCA with the mission of increasing the knowledge and skills available to meet critical problems in the LDCs, including those at the middle-income level. It would work with U.S. institutions and their counterparts in the LDCs. In principle, it would be different from AID in having a long-term, problem-oriented focus rather than a short-term, country-oriented one, and it would involve the LDCs in the planning and programming functions. According to plans, the ISTC's operating style will be less formal and complicated and more direct and collaborative than AID's.

University Involvement in Development Assistance

The ISTC may come into being as a new agency whether or not AID is reorganized, and if so it would make a major contribution to the scientific and technological development of the LDCs. Among its antecedents is the study by Harrington (1978), whose chief concerns were strengthening international programs and exchanges, expanding long-term cooperative relationships between American universities and the LDCs (including the middle-income LDCs), and securing more federal support for these endeavors. In 1977, Harrington's project resulted in a preliminary agreement by the major professional associations in higher education to set up a new organization, the Council for International Cooperation in Higher Education (CICHE). It was to serve as a clearinghouse on international cooperation and was intended to strengthen relationships between U.S. and foreign organizations. However, despite the substantial funding and staff resources devoted to the planning of the new organization, it failed to get under way, largely because the final plans were unjustifiably elaborate and expensive.

Discussions of the proposal to establish CICHE focused on the issue of what kinds of American postsecondary institutions should participate in development assistance and how they might benefit from CICHE's existence. Some of its supporters looked to the concept of international linkages in higher education as a way of getting a wider range of postsecondary institutions to participate in development assistance. Thus far, the major research and land-grant universities have been most active in this field. In 1976-77, of the 68 universities with AID contracts in agriculture and rural development, 46 were land-grant universities (National Association of State Universities and Land-Grant Colleges [NASULC], 1978a).

A 1975 survey of the 300 members of the American Association of State Colleges and Universities (AASCU) indicated that only 17 of them, or about 5 percent, had development-assistance contracts with LDCs (Gray, 1977). Less than one-fourth of the members of the American Association of Colleges for Teacher Education (AACTE) whose international activities were surveyed in 1968-71 had such contracts (Klassen, Imig, and Yff, 1973). But it is striking that these institutions were especially active in international-education programs of all kinds: They accounted for 64 percent of the work done in curriculum materials development, 70 percent of the research in international education, and 90 percent of the special training seminars and courses provided for foreigners in the United States. It is conjectured that this level of international activity developed, *inter alia,* from changes in faculty perspectives resulting from international experience (Klassen, Imig, and Yff, 1973).

The differing involvement of various kinds of institutions in development assistance has been largely a matter of their resources and programs, the accessibility and relevance of the programs to the LDCs, and institutional commitment. Important in connection with this last item is how an institution's involvement in development assistance relates to its other activities. As Harvard President Derek Bok (1977, p. 34) has noted, "service activities in a university are unlikely to remain at a high level of quality for very long unless they reinforce the regular teaching and research of the institution . . . rather than diffusing the energies of the faculty over too broad a terrain."

The code of practice drafted by the National Association of State Universities and Land-Grant Colleges may be particularly timely in this connection (NASULC, 1978b). Among other things, it sets forth standards for the participation of higher-education institutions in development assistance. The proposed code affirms that colleges and universities should not engage in international activities for missionary or monetary purposes. They should take on such activities only if they can be integrated into the institution's overall mission and only if the faculty reward system and administrative structure give priority to international activities and the entire curriculum can take on a more international perspective. In other words, the international projects of American colleges and universities should not be an isolated activity of the faculty members involved; rather, they should be part of a commitment that is central to the aims of the institution and in keeping with its administrative structure. Furthermore, as C. Peter Magrath, President of the University of Minnesota, has stated, the common attitude toward international programs by university administrations—"we love them but we don't fund them"—must change; verbal commitments to international programs must be backed up with real funds (Magrath, 1978).

8

Advanced Training and Research: Background and Current Situation

Since Lambert's 1973 study, there has been no comparable analysis of the state of advanced international and area studies and research in the United States. However, several studies in this field were under way in mid-1979. The Ford Foundation was assessing the prospects of international studies, primarily in the major research universities, and the probable effects of national research awards on those prospects. The President's Commission on Foreign Language and International Studies was gathering voluminous data on international- and area-studies centers and had commissioned several major studies, including a largely qualitative analysis by the Rand Corporation of the national market for people with foreign-language and international-studies training. Commission consultant Roger Paget undertook a review of the state of international and area studies, focusing on the junior level of graduate studies and based on site visits to some 40 institutions other than the major research universities.

These and other studies should significantly advance the available knowledge in this complex field and assist the President's commission in determining its recommendations in this area. Since the results of these studies are available only in a preliminary form at this time, my chief objective is to provide general background and to identify some of the major issues involved in graduate international and area studies (including foreign languages) and research.

The Development of International and Area Studies

In the wake of World War II, American higher education offered almost no courses dealing with Asia, Africa, or the Middle East —except in the classics—and the situation was little better with respect to Latin America and the Soviet Union. The resulting shortage of Americans with expertise in these areas to serve on foreign-affairs staffs led to pressure for radical changes in American higher education.

The Carnegie Corporation and the Rockefeller Foundation were the first to attempt to remedy this situation—for example, by supporting Russian studies at Columbia and Harvard, Japanese studies at the University of Michigan, and African studies at Northwestern University. Although in terms of scale their contributions were not at the level of later Ford Foundation support, in relation to their resources they were generous as well as timely.

In 1952, the Ford Foundation inaugurated its Foreign Area Fellowship Program to support advanced graduate training on non-Western regions, the Soviet Union, and Eastern Europe (around 2,050 fellowships between 1952 and 1967) and eventually on Western Europe. During its existence, the Foundation's International Training and Research (ITR) program provided major grants to some 30 universities for the development of graduate training and research programs in area and international studies; support for the development of undergraduate international studies in over 100 colleges; research grants to national organizations such as the Social Science Research Council, the American Council of Learned Societies, and the Center for Applied Linguistics (CAL); and support for functional fields —first law and later various other professions. ITR's support was extremely important in encouraging catalytic, clearinghouse, and interface functions, as in its support of Education and World Affairs and the Midwest Universities Consortium for International Activities. When the ITR program came to an end in 1967 (the final grants expired in 1972), there were over 40 major centers of advanced training and research in international and area studies, and some 30 universities had received substantial foundation support. Together with the Carnegie Corporation and the Rockefeller Foundation, the Ford Foundation had produced the base for area and international studies so notably lacking in the early postwar period.

Paralleling the Ford Foundation's ITR program was the federal government's effort to support foreign languages and other critical subjects under the Sputnik-prompted National Defense Education Act of 1958. Title VI of NDEA authorized programs for foreign-language and area studies in order to increase the national pool of specialists in foreign languages, area studies, and world affairs and to update the knowledge of existing specialists; to produce new knowledge about other nations—especially non-Western ones—through research and development; and to develop improved curricula and instructional materials. The emphasis of NDEA Title VI, which is administered by OE, was on U.S. national-defense needs. Table 1 is a breakdown of Title VI funding.

From its inception until 1978-79, a total of $229.1 million was spent on NDEA Title VI (U.S. General Accounting Office [GAO], 1978b), or around $11 million per year, compared with the average of $18 million per year spent on the Ford Foundation's 15-year ITR program. But Title VI funding has undergone various shifts and only escaped serious reductions— or total elimination—because in every year except 1970, Congress appropriated more funds than the executive branch requested. The record since 1970 is shown in Table 2.

In terms of constant dollars, the funding for Title VI has decreased by over 40 percent since 1967 (when the actual dollar amount was $13 million) to $7.68 million in fiscal year 1978. The impact of this major decrease in funding on Title VI programs has been exacerbated by the unpredictability of the funding. The first and most dramatic instance of this was the drastic

Table 1. Breakdown of NDEA Title VI funding

Program funded	Total number		Program objectives	Cost ($ millions)		
	FY 77	FY 78		FY 77	FY 78	From inception (1958) through FY 1978
Centers for international, language, and area studies	80	80	Advanced training in languages not traditionally taught in U.S. and area studies of issues related to major world regions.	$ 7.9	$ 8.0	$ 81.0
International studies						
Graduate programs	13	13	To encourage cooperation between international studies and professional programs and to bring a comparative dimension to professional school instruction.	0.5	0.5	3.5
Undergraduate programs	25	25	Innovative programs to strengthen international studies in general education, especially at the lower-division level.	0.8	0.9	5.2
Fellowships (graduate level)	830	828	Fellowships for graduate students to attend NDEA Title VI centers of institutions offering international studies programs for up to a cumulative total of 48 months.	4.5	4.6	88.0
Research	34	35	Primarily, developing teaching materials for non-Western languages; also teaching methodology and state-of-the-art surveys of foreign-language and area and international studies.	0.9	1.0	47.3
				$14.6	$15.0	$229.1[a]

[a]Includes $4 million for intensive summer language programs, discontinued after FY 1972.

Source: Data obtained from U.S. Department of Health, Education, and Welfare, Office of Education.

Table 2. Congressional Title VI appropriations
($ millions)

Fiscal year	Authorized	Requested	Congressional appropriation	Appropriation differential
1970	$30.0	$15.0	$13.0	$ −2.0
1971	38.5	4.93	7.17	2.24
1972	38.5	13.94	13.94	0
1973	50.0	1.00	12.525	11.525
1974	75.0	0	11.333	11.333
1975	75.0	8.64	11.3	2.66
1976	75.0	8.64	13.3	4.66
1977	75.0	8.64	14.65	6.01
1978	75.0	13.3	15.0	1.7
1979	75.0	15.0	17.0	2.0

Source: U.S. General Accounting Office, 1978b, p. 13; Gould, 1979, p. 4.

decrease in Title VI centers in 1973-74, from 106 to 50. (They have since increased to 80, situated at 43 institutions.)

The sharp reduction in centers resulted from the 1972 Title VI Amendments, which removed the requirement that language training be a component of a center's activities and permitted two new kinds of programs: (1) graduate international-studies programs oriented toward contemporary problems or topics such as the environment, and (2) undergraduate international-studies programs to add an international perspective to general education, especially lower-division collegiate programs. The graduate programs, by regulation, must include coverage of more than one area of the world, must be of contemporary relevance, and must be comparative and/or interdisciplinary in approach. The graduate programs are often based in professional schools. (The innovative character of undergraduate programs was described in Chapter 3.)

These new, so-called exemplary programs ("exemplary" because they were to initiate new approaches that would be replicable at other higher-education institutions) reflected an administration decision to disperse Title VI funding more widely in order to encourage the greater institutional initiative anticipated in the unfunded International Education Act of 1966. Additional factors may have included a feeling that the center program had fulfilled its goals along with disenchantment on the part of the administration with the established Title VI centers because of the antiadministration stance of many center staff at the height of the Vietnam War.

The impact of the Lambert study (1973) cannot be underestimated. Lambert indirectly recommended diversification of Title VI centers; specifically, he called for a limited number of large, multipurpose centers and other specialized ones, more attention to international studies in undergraduate education, and more intercenter coordination or consortial arrangements. Although he did not explicitly recommend a structured hierarchy, he seemed to deplore the tendency of every center to aspire to the status of a major center, as well as the fact that NDEA funding encouraged centers "to think of themselves largely as the producers of graduate specialists" (Lambert, 1973, p. 406).

As the exemplary new programs were on the verge of being launched, the administration cut the fiscal year 1973 Title VI budget request to zero. Funding was not restored until June 30, too late for intensive language programs to be offered that summer. After that, with diminished Title VI funding, it seemed impossible to revive the summer program, although centers can—and often do—use their grants for summer program salaries, and Title VI regulations explicitly authorize centers to use their federal funds for summer language programs.

With the demise (for all practical purposes) of the summer language program came the end of summer foreign-language fellowships. Together, the annual NDEA and summer language fellowships had totaled around 2,400 in 1969-70; of these, about 1,300 were summer-only fellowships, and some 1,100 were Foreign Language and Area Studies (FLAS) fellowships. Statistics citing a drop in NDEA fellowships from around 2,400 in 1969-70 to 817 in 1973-74 are, thus, grossly misleading. The number of FLAS fellowships has decreased—from a high of some 1,100 to around 830—a decrease caused largely by rising tuition costs.

The new undergraduate and graduate studies programs shot up from 18 to 75 in 1972-73 for the reasons just mentioned: many of the centers whose funding terminated that year applied for support under the new programs. Then they dropped to 38 in 1975-76, remaining at around that number since then. Tables 3 and 4 present information on Title VI centers, programs, and fellowships and the area distribution of the centers.

Table 3. NDEA centers, programs, and fellowships, 1959-1979

Fiscal year	Centers	Graduate programs	Undergraduate programs	Fellowships	Funding ($ millions)
1959-60	19				
1960-61	46				
1961-62	52				
1962-63	53				
1963-64	55				
1965-66	98				
1967-68	106				
1969-70	107			ca. 2400	
1971-72	106			1755	
1972-73	106	6	12	1028	
1973-74	50	25	50	817	
1974-75	50	23	50	835	$4.65
1975-76	66[a]	11	27	763	$5.77
1976-77	80[b]	12	28	842	$7.24
1977-78	80[b]	13	24	832	$7.90
1978-79	80[b]	13	25	828	$8.00

[a]Includes 9 undergraduate centers.

[b]Includes 15 undergraduate centers.

Source: Data obtained from U.S. Department of Health, Education, and Welfare, Office of Education.

Two additional changes in Title VI in the 1970s significantly altered the basic programs: the requirements of "out-

Table 4. Subject area distribution, Title VI centers, 1973-1979

Subject area	1973-74	1974-75	1975-76	1976-77	1977-78	1978-79
East Asia	8	8	15	15	15	15
South Asia	6	6	6	8	8	8
Southeast Asia	3	3	3	3	3	3
Middle East	7	7	11	12	12	12
Russia and Eastern Europe	8	8	13	14	14	14
Africa	6	6	6	8	8	8
Latin America	6	6	6	10	10	10
General[a]	6	6	6	10	10	10
Total	50	50	66	80	80	80

[a]Comparative and general, Inner Asia, Pacific Islands, Western Europe, Canada.

Source: Data obtained from U.S. Department of Health, Education, and Welfare, Office of Education.

reach" activities and the so-called citizen-education amendment to Title VI (these were discussed in Chapter 3.) Since 1978, OE has demanded that international-studies centers devote the equivalent of at least 15 percent of their federal funds to outreach activities. This requirement is intended to stimulate all centers to engage in activities that use the resources developed in the core program to strengthen international education in other institutions or agencies. Each center is expected to plan its outreach activities in relation to its resources and the needs in its area (*Federal Register,* 1977, p. 26207).

Many centers strongly resent the outreach requirement, claiming that it diverts them from what they consider their primary function, namely, advanced training and research. University faculty do not claim or seek expertise in working with schools and community groups, nor is such activity rewarded with promotion or tenure. Therefore, many centers staff their outreach activities with graduate students, a system that ensures lack of continuity of management. The outreach requirement is also problematic because of the virtual impossibility of auditing the 15 percent equivalent and because a center can claim that it is fulfilling the requirement without undertaking programs that are significantly different from its normal offerings. The fact that the centers seem to get mixed signals from OE on the priority they should give to outreach activities aggravates the situation and reinforces the centers' ambivalence. (A number of centers, it should be emphasized, enthusiastically support the outreach concept and mount impressive programs.)

The citizen-education amendment of 1976 (which added Section 603 to NDEA Title VI) received the endorsement of many Title VI center and program staff members, at least publicly. In theory, the programs eligible for funding under Section 603 presented no threat to higher-education centers because a "trigger" mechanism (described in Chapter 3) assures existing centers and programs of at least $15 million before Section 603 can be funded. However, established centers and programs have become increasingly fearful that the imminent reauthorization of NDEA Title VI may remove the trigger, thereby opening up competition for Title VI funds between existing centers and programs and other school and community organizations that are active in international education.

The defensive attitude of international-studies faculty can be explained by their experience with Title VI. The combination of the drastic reduction in centers and the termination of intensive summer language programs and fellowships in 1973-74, the precariousness of Title VI funding from year to year, the reduction of over 40 percent (in constant dollars) in Title VI funds since 1967, the diversification of the program to include the graduate and undergraduate programs and the outreach requirement, and finally the prospect that the "trigger" may be removed from Section 603—all of these have been seen as a case of robbing Peter to pay Paul in a zero-sum game. Decreasing funds have been diverted in more directions, at times erratically. The fact that, in the 1960s, the emphasis of both the Ford Foundation and NDEA support was on specialized advanced training, primarily at the doctoral level, contributed to the impression of a lack of a coherent rationale in the directions taken by Title VI in the 1970s and to the feeling that departures from basic specialist training inevitably involve dilution of quality and the denigration of area studies as such—even though the new program directions have been needed and timely. This situation, aggravated by what appear to be overly bureaucratic demands by OE, has not made for the best relations between OE and the centers. Yet, despite these difficulties, NDEA Title VI has resulted in important accomplishments, as the next section indicates.

The Effects of NDEA Title VI
on Area and International Studies

According to a U.S. General Accounting Office study (1978b), NDEA center programs produced 63,240 B.A.'s, 23,590 M.A.'s, and 8,620 Ph.D.'s between 1959 and 1976. These figures are calculated on the basis of center participants with a minimum of 15 credit hours in language and area training, including (since 1973) the general international-studies category. In 1978-79, Title VI funded 80 international and area-studies centers and an additional 13 graduate and 25 undergraduate exemplary programs. The graduate/undergraduate centers cost an average of $109,000 annually and enrolled a total of 64,000 students. Undergraduate center costs averaged $50,000 per center, with total enrollments of 14,000. The graduate and undergraduate programs cost an average of $40,000 and $33,000, respectively. Estimated enrollment in the latter is 35,000 for all 25 programs (that is, for the 10 to 12 courses in each program that typically enroll large numbers of undergraduate students) (U.S. DHEW, 1978b).

NDEA Title VI funds, together with major foundation support, have been essential to the development and maintenance of international and area studies. It should be emphasized, however, that federal funds constitute only a small portion of international-studies center budgets—9.05 percent in 1976-77 and 9.1 percent in 1978-79 (Schneider, 1978)—though they may constitute close to half of the budgets of international-studies programs. Nevertheless, these funds have given the centers and programs significant leverage in securing other financial support. The growing pressure on higher-education resources in the past few years has made federal dollars even more important to

NDEA centers. This is so even though, for the most part, these funds are no longer used to support full-time tenured staff (they may be paying partial salaries to tenure-track faculty). Instead, they are generally used to pay for released time from teaching for designing new courses or administrative duties and for language instruction—especially at the advanced levels of the less commonly taught languages—which, because of high cost and low enrollments, can rarely be self-supporting.

A 1977 report on Japanese studies in the United States (Massey and Massey, 1977) affirms the important contribution of Title VI to advanced training and research in this field. The report distinguishes between "complete graduate programs" and "limited graduate programs." Criteria for the former include Japanese language library holdings of 25,000 or more volumes; courses dealing exclusively with Japan offered in four or more disciplines; a minimum of eight faculty specialists on Japan; language offerings at all levels; and a strong commitment to Japanese studies from at least four disciplines in addition to those that offer courses dealing exclusively with Japan. Such programs increased from 11 in 1969-70 to 15 in 1974-75. All but two were supported by Title VI; and only one graduate Title VI East Asian Center was not among these "complete" programs. Federal funding in Japanese studies thus correlates closely with program strength. From 1945 to 1974, of the doctorates awarded for dissertations dealing primarily with Japan, 65.8 percent were awarded by 12 of the 15 East Asia programs now supported by NDEA, further confirming its contribution (Massey and Massey, 1977).

Also largely to the credit of federal (and Ford Foundation) support of area studies is the existence of a substantial pool of specialists on the Soviet Union and Eastern Europe. Preliminary results of the first stage of the "Dynamic Inventory of Soviet and East European Studies in the United States," a project of the American Association for the Advancement of Slavic Studies (AAASS), suggest that there are close to 10,000 such specialists (self-identified), or four times the current membership of the AAASS. Data gathered in this three-year AAASS project, which was initiated in 1977 and is funded by OE, will eventually reveal the role of Title VI (and other programs) in the production of these specialists as well as their employment record. It will indicate how many are or have been at Title VI centers as students, faculty, or researchers; the extent to which specialists have dropped out of the field or applied their specialized training in their professional life, and much else (Eason, 1977, 1978). So far it appears that, at a very rough estimate, at least one-fourth of self-defined specialists on the Soviet Union and Eastern Europe are the products of Title VI programs. The extension of such an inventory to other area-studies fields is obviously important in assessing the supply of and demand for specialists and in identifying the support needed for area and international studies nationally—the topics of later sections of this chapter and the next.

Overall, Title VI has been remarkably successful. It has produced an impressive pool of area and international specialists and provided international education to many thousands of undergraduates. By the mid-1970s, nearly 90 percent of former NDEA Title VI fellows used their area training in their first job (more recent data are not available). NDEA has been crucial in library acquisitions in international area studies (11.1 percent of center budgets for 1978-79 were allocated to this purpose; Schneider, 1978), and by May 1978, the Language and Area Studies Research program had produced some 850 major reports on surveys and studies, instructional materials for language and area studies, and 500 related publications. In short, the achievements of Title VI have been impressive.

NDEA Title VI and Foreign-Language Study

A major effect of NDEA Title VI has been to strengthen foreign-language study, especially in the less commonly taught languages. Over 80 languages have been designated as priority languages for Title VI funding by the Commissioner of Education since 1959. In 1976-77, a total of 92 modern and 16 ancient languages were offered at NDEA centers.

Title VI Foreign Language and Area Studies (FLAS) Fellowships (originally called National Defense Foreign-Language Fellowships) contribute to foreign-language study by supporting graduate students in foreign-language studies, area studies, and (since 1974) international studies. The fellowships are awarded to higher-education institutions, mainly but not exclusively those with NDEA centers. (In 1978-79, one-fifth of the institutions that were awarded FLAS quotas did not have NDEA centers.) To be eligible for a FLAS quota allocation, an institution must offer foreign-language training, a requirement that applies to general international-studies programs (none had received a FLAS quota by 1979) as well as area centers. Institutions receiving a FLAS quota recruit and screen applications for fellowships and then nominate candidates to OE, which selects the fellows and alternates from among those candidates.

The allocation of fellowships to specific institutions has been criticized for ensuring financial support (fellows' tuition and fees) to those institutions and depriving other institutions of this advantage and for limiting the fellows' institutional choices. However, letting individuals take their fellowships to any institution they wish would probably result in a greater concentration of fellows at fewer institutions than now obtains. Critics also attack the fact that NDEA fellows can take their awards abroad only if they are in an approved overseas language-training center; however, this criticism neglects the absence in the NDEA system of adequate standards for assessing the feasibility and political sensitivity of fellows' proposed projects or studies abroad. The more appropriate response to this criticism would be to expand the overseas Fulbright programs of OE and ICA.

A legitimate concern relating to NDEA fellowships is the Title VI requirement of "reasonable assurance that the recipients of such stipends will, on completion of their training, be available for teaching service . . . or such other service of a public nature as may be permitted in the regulations of the Secretary." With the decreasing number of teaching opportunities for area specialists, this limitation appears unrealistic. Furthermore, the regulations are so general that the restriction may be meaningless; "other service of a public nature" is defined as employment with federal, state, or local governments, international organizations in which the United States participates, or nonprofit, nonsectarian organizations, the activities of which contribute significantly to the conduct of United States foreign relations, or other employment that will contribute to the nation's cultural, educational, or scientific understanding of other countries (*Federal Register,* 1977, pp. 26212-26213).

College and university enrollments in the less commonly taught languages, in contrast to the commonly taught ones, have increased substantially—from 12,099 in 1960 to 63,928 in 1977 (U.S. General Accounting Office, 1978b). These figures include 187 languages, not just the 108 offered at NDEA centers. However, enrollments vary greatly among even the major languages, and in some languages they have been declining. The cost of language instruction when only a handful of students are involved is difficult for colleges and universities to absorb. Furthermore, the problem mentioned earlier of measuring language learning by achieved competency rather than by hours spent in the classroom is probably more critical with the less commonly taught languages than with the commonly taught ones, because courses with low enrollments are often taught only in alternate years, so that students do not have an uninterrupted sequence of courses. Finally, advanced materials are lacking in many of the less commonly taught languages, and self-instructional programs now rarely go beyond the beginning level—yet another area that clearly needs much more development.

The national need in terms of the less commonly taught languages includes not only achieving substantial enrollments but also ensuring a sufficient pool of people who are proficient in most of the world's languages. Richard Lambert recently elaborated on this point (1978, pp. 4-5): "No one knows what the attrition rate is of existing specialists losing their competencies. The evidence . . . indicates a genuine need to upgrade the competencies, particularly the language competencies, of a substantial portion of existing specialists . . . . The OE-NDEA VI orientation is geared to the provision of new language skills and new specialists. No one, so far as I know, is concerned with the retention of language skills once gained." Lambert is now engaged in a long-term study of foreign-language competency—

both maintenance and attrition—funded by the National Endowment for the Humanities (NEH). This should be important in tracking specialists and identifying what is needed to maintain competency in a foreign language. The eventual recommendations of this study will undoubtedly merit support.

The MLA Task Force on the Less Commonly Taught Languages (MLA, 1979) produced a series of recommendations. It urged enrollment targets in postsecondary education of 100,000 each for four "wide-use" languages—those serving as a medium of wider communication for major areas of the world, that is, Arabic, Chinese, Japanese, and Russian—by 1987-88. For other languages, it urged an increase in current enrollment levels of anywhere from 100 to 1,000 percent "in response to perceived needs and pressures in each individual case." These goals are set forth in Table 5. Other task force recommendations focused on individualized and self-instructional programs, materials development, summer institutes and fellowships, and study-abroad programs.

Table 5. Postsecondary institutions offering less commonly taught
languages and enrollments in 1974 (actual) and 1988 (projected)

	1974 institutions (actual)			1988 institutions (goal)		
	Four-year	Two-year	Enrollment	Four-year	Two-year	Enrollment
Russian	486	75	32,522	1,500	500	100,000
Chinese	163	18	10,576	1,500	500	100,000
Japanese	139	27	9,604	1,500	500	100,000
Arabic	77	4	2,034	1,500	500	100,000
Hebrew	260	19	22,371	350	60	30,000
Portuguese	139	7	5,073	350	50	25,000
Hindi-Urdu	32	—	384	200	20	15,000
Polish	48	3	1,123	160	50	5,000
Serbo-Croatian	24	—	242	160	50	5,000
Persian	18	—	278	160	50	5,000

(continued on next page)

Table 5 *(Continued)*

	1974 institutions (actual)			1988 institutions (goal)		
	Four-year	Two-year	Enroll-ment	Four-year	Two-year	Enroll-ment
Turkish	21	1	156	160	50	5,000
Swahili	58	12	1,694	160	50	5,000
Indonesian	13	—	134	160	50	5,000
Norwegian	29	3	1,557	120	20	3,000
Swedish	40	6	1,396	120	20	3,000
Modern Greek	24	1	533	120	20	3,000
Hausa	8	—	46	120	20	3,000
Bengali	6	—	27	120	20	3,000
Yiddish	22	—	1,079	60	20	3,000
Czech	19	2	337	45	5	1,000
Ukrainian	12	1	117	45	5	1,000
Korean	8	—	87	45	5	1,000
Dutch	20	1	456	45	5	1,000
Cantonese	3	—	46	20	—	500
Amharic	2	—	8	20	—	500
Mandingo	0	—	0	20	—	500
Ngala	0	—	0	20	—	500
Hungarian	8	—	64	20	—	500
Romanian	8	—	31	20	—	500
Bulgarian	3	—	4	20	—	500
Finnish	7	2	134	20	—	500
Armenian	6	1	121	20	—	500
Pashto	0	—	0	20	—	500
Oromo	0	—	0	20	—	500
Yoruba	7	—	87	20	—	500
Igbo	1	—	2	20	—	500
Tigrena	0	—	0	20	—	500
Fula	0	—	0	20	—	500
Thai	8	—	71	20	—	500
Vietnamese	6	—	29	20	—	500
Burmese	1	—	4	20	—	500
Danish	13	—	183	20	—	500

Source: Modern Language Association (MLA), 1979.

The final report of the task force affirms the objectives set forth for enrollments by 1988 in the less commonly taught languages. Considering the paucity of current enrollments in major wide-use languages, these objectives are not unreasonable and may indeed be modest when looked at in the context of the need for the United States to understand and communicate with an enormous range of countries whose populations speak one of the less commonly taught languages. However, decisions to expand the teaching of foreign languages significantly at the advanced level, including the less commonly taught languages, must come to grips with the problem of limited employment opportunities for foreign-language specialists, a subject discussed in the next chapter.

The Current State of Foreign-Area and International-Affairs Research

NDEA Title VI, Section 601, authorizes the funding of "research and training in international studies and the international aspects of professional and other fields of study." In principle, therefore, the NDEA centers can undertake foreign-area and international-affairs research. Guidelines in the 1977 *Federal Register* (p. 26211) however, state that "funds awarded under this subpart [allowable costs] may not be used for . . . center research." In practice, the research prohibited by this statement is major research projects—for example, of a team or collaborative nature—and the individual research projects of center faculty are not prohibited. Not surprisingly, the guidelines are interpreted as excluding even individual research (considerable investigation is needed in order to learn what they do and do not prohibit), and as a consequence center faculty tend not to look to Title VI to support research beyond what is possible under such rubrics as travel, administrative costs, library acquisitions, graduate student assistantships, and conference attendance, all of which contribute importantly to research. The Title VI research that is explicitly funded involves chiefly foreign-language teaching materials and studies on teaching methodology and the state of language, area, and international studies.

The phrase "foreign-affairs-related research" is used here to refer to research on foreign societies and international relations, both broadly conceived. It involves mainly the social and behavioral sciences and denotes faculty and other forms of research, essentially postdoctoral. It includes support for released time for faculty to do research, for the postdoctoral research of young scholars, for fieldwork, for publication activities, and for the acquisition and maintenance of library collections.

Because of the spiraling costs of foreign-area library collections, and because these are crucial to area research, a major effort is needed at the national level to sustain them. Such collections have grown impressively in the past 20 years with foundation and federal support. But with the termination of substantial foundation funding and the erosion of federal money (in constant dollars), the maintenance of these collections is threatened. Area-studies collections are particularly vulnerable to budget cuts by universities because of their high unit costs and low rate of use. The time is long past—if it ever existed—when a single institution could collect everything. Increased cooperation among major repositories will be essential in the future for the acquisition, processing, and servicing of foreign materials, especially because of the decentralized structure of the library system in the United States. (The outstanding report of the American Council on Education [1975b], *Library Resources for International Education,* addressed this issue eloquently.) Support for foreign-affairs-related research should include both substantial subsidies to collections designated as national or regional repositories and national leadership in support of a system for sharing the costs of and access to major collections.

The federal funding of foreign-affairs-related contract and grant research declined from $40.6 million by 26 agencies in 1967-68 to around $32.6 million by 20 agencies in 1976-77. In constant dollars, the decrease was 52 percent. As roughly half of this goes to the universities, federal funding of foreign-affairs research in the universities went down from $20.3 million to $8.5 million (in constant dollars) in this period. Four agencies contributed 74.5 percent of the support in fiscal year 1976:

AID, the Department of Defense, DHEW, and the National Science Foundation ("Ten Years . . . ," 1977).

Between fiscal years 1972 and 1976, federal support of foreign-area research in centers at universities classified by the Carnegie system as research universities decreased by 5.6 percent (in constant dollars), while the corresponding decrease in foundation funding for this research was 36.9 percent (Atelsek and Gomberg, 1976). The foundations, especially the Ford Foundation, retreated from this field in the late 1960s, when it appeared that the new International Education Act would take over the major responsibility. Today "no major federal program or collection of programs across agencies exists to fill the financial gap left by the pullback of Ford Foundation and other private and institutionally based support" (American Council on Education, 1977, p. 7).

Advanced foreign-affairs research in the universities is crucial for several reasons. It is essential to strengthen and advance scholarship. It is also vital to the national interest because of the importance of a vigorous dialectic relationship between the nation's private research capabilities and its government research, and policymaking, and implementing capabilities. In the words of E. Raymond Platig, Director of the Office of External Research in the Department of State, "Assuming that it is the human condition to live with imperfect knowledge, imperfect policy, and imperfect coordination of the two, there is still a good case to be made for the proposition that, other things being equal, more knowledgeable policymakers produce sounder policy. Thus, on national policy grounds alone the nation has an interest in the private centers and programs of advanced research."[1]

The maintenance of a strong private-sector capability in advanced foreign-affairs research is needed even with a sufficient supply of area- and international-studies specialists in the pipeline. Continuing basic research cannot be carried out by the federal intelligence establishment, because its research is dominated by short-term deadlines and the immediate demands

[1]E. Raymond Platig to Barbara B. Burn, June 16, 1978.

stemming from current intelligence issues. It must therefore draw upon the research carried on in universities—their intellectual and analytical capital—for both substance and perspective.

According to 15 university presidents, research universities are "of critical importance not just to the university world but to the quality and even the security of American life" (Ford Foundation, 1978, p. 12). They urged a 10-year program of federal grants to strengthen university research on foreign areas and international problems. Substantially increased support has also been urged by Ward (1977, p. 14) as essential to "the nation's genuine international competence."

Basic research must be undertaken not just in universities but also in private research firms and at overseas centers for advanced research. These include the Universities Service Center in Hong Kong, the American Academy in Rome, the American Institute of Indian Studies, and other centers located in Italy, Greece, and the Middle East. Diverse in their origins, facilities, and programs, these centers share a commitment to scholarship on other countries and cultures, scholarship that feeds into international studies at all levels of American education.

Most of the centers focus more on the humanities than on the social sciences. Some concentrate more on earlier periods than on the contemporary world. They are important in training academically competent regional specialists and promoting international cultural and intellectual contacts. The Universities Service Center has played a central role in research on contemporary China; all American scholars in Chinese studies have spent time at the center.

These overseas research centers face a perilous financial future because of inflation, declining foreign-exchange rates, the diminution of PL 480 funds, decreased foundation giving, and the increased pressures on American higher-education institutions. The American Academy of Arts and Sciences has carried out a major study of these centers as part of a coordinated attempt to ensure adequate funding for an important element in the total system of international research. As of this writing, the results of this study have not yet been published.

The gravity of the continuing decline in foreign-area research, especially on the Soviet Union and Eastern Europe, was the focus of a seminar held at the Georgetown University Center for Strategic and International Studies in April 1977. The summary of the seminar discussion affirmed the urgent need for increased support: "The problems faced by universities, government agencies, and research firms stem from the lack of prominence, or even sustained interest, given to the field of foreign area research—and significantly even to that of research on the U.S.S.R. and Eastern Europe. The major thrust of the discussion in this seminar was on the problems of maintaining and reenergizing research efforts focusing on the U.S.S.R. and Eastern Europe. However, to solve the problems in these areas, the practical answer is to solve the basic needs for the entire field of foreign area research" (Sullivan, 1977, p. 22).

Although quantifying the level of federal funds needed for foreign-affairs research, like quantifying the number of specialists needed, is extremely difficult, the consensus of a number of authorities is a level of $10-15 million per year. This would provide average annual grants of about $100,000 to $150,000 to up to 100 centers and programs to cover part or all of the following costs: (1) stipends for individuals engaged in postdoctoral or comparable advanced research; (2) released time for postdoctoral research by regular faculty members; and (3) such direct costs as acquiring and servicing research materals; salaries and benefits for library, secretarial, and research support staff; and the costs of acquiring office equipment, supplies, and communications.

A major weakness in the funding of foreign-affairs-related research is its structure. A recent development in this area was the formation in February 1978 of the National Council for Soviet and East European Research. The purpose of the council, which is an autonomous academic body, is "to develop and sustain a long-term, substantial and high-quality program of fundamental research dealing with major policy issues and questions of Soviet and East European social, political, economic, and historical development" (Sullivan, 1977, p. 22). The council was formed through the collaborative efforts of senior officials of 10 universities, the American Association for the Advancement of Slavic Studies, and the Kennan Institute for Advanced Russian Studies. Its initial funding consisted of $500,000 from the Department of Defense.

The ideal model for federal funding of advanced foreign-affairs research has been much debated. While OE might seem to be a possibility because it administers NDEA Title VI and related activities, its research mission is education, not foreign affairs. Because the National Science Foundation and the National Endowment for the Humanities are concerned, respectively, with the social and hard sciences and humanities (and foreign-affairs research encompasses both), neither agency is entirely appropriate as the research funding agency. The Department of State and the International Communication Agency would both face concern about academic freedom and integrity, because they are mission-directed organizations. Given these difficulties, a possible arrangement might be an organization comparable in some ways to Britain's University Grants Committee or the National Endowment for the Humanities: autonomous, supported by public funds, and organized to function through a peer review system similar to that of the National Science Foundation. A new, separate organization would, however, face many obstacles, not the least of which would be the difficulty of establishing a new agency and its lack of leverage with limited funds.

The structure of funding for international-studies research is one of the thornier issues facing the president's commission. Perhaps more difficult, however, is the problem of determining the kinds and levels of activities that international- and area-studies centers and programs should carry out—and with what level of federal subsidy—and how to strike the appropriate balance between what the national interest requires and what "consumers" of international expertise perceive as their needs in terms of knowledge and trained people. The next chapter addresses some of these issues.

9

Advanced Training and Research: Needs and Future Directions

The Need for Specialists

Lambert (1973) projected a need both within and outside of the academic world of around 13,000 additional language and area specialists with Ph.D.'s for the 1970-80 period. It is estimated that the number of Ph.D.'s actually produced between 1969 and 1979 doubled the supply then available to around 17,500, of whom around 9,000 are in higher education. However, Lambert's estimates did not take into account the major decrease in funding for international and area studies in the 1970s, the impact of leveling higher-education enrollments, and the negative attitudes toward international studies generated by the Vietnam war.

The fundamental issue of how much international/area studies is enough has long defied solution. With the diminution of both foundation and governmental funding, this issue has grown increasingly acute. The General Accounting Office (GAO), in its report, *Study of Foreign Languages and Related Areas,* retreated from the issue on the ground that "there is no standard definition of a specialist" (U.S. GAO, 1978b, p. 17).

The GAO expressed the view that, because specialists cannot be defined, the need for them and the cost of the system required to produce them elude quantification. It concluded (p. 29): "During the last several years, the Congress has provided a stable level of federal funding with slight increases to offset inflation. No convincing case has been made known to us for increasing or decreasing this funding level."

As the GAO observed, "specialists" in language and area studies (as in art, musicology, environmental sciences, and so on) vary greatly. Just as there should be diversity in the aims and programs of international-studies centers, so should there be diversity in the training and professional roles of their product. Lambert (1973) found that only 11.5 percent of the 1957-1959 graduates of the top-quality area programs were employed by these programs in 1967-1969, the rest being dispersed through a range of institutions and in the nonacademic world as well, thus affirming the need for different kinds of specialization and employment expectations. The continued need for diversity is reflected by the facts that close to half of the current Ph.D.'s in international/area studies are in fields other than higher education and that two-thirds of those in higher education are at a variety of institutions rather than being concentrated at the major research universities.

The lack of a precise definition of area- and international-studies specialists, together with the absence of firm data on employment needs for them, undoubtedly complicates the problem of determining the appropriate level of federal and other support for advanced training and research in this field. But it is not necessary to abandon the task simply because much of it cannot be quantified. For one thing, employment prospects for international-studies graduates are only one factor in determining output. A major function of programs and centers is to teach undergraduate students, a function that has received increased emphasis in the late 1970s. Another essential function is the production of scholarly research.

Related to the production of research is the wider need to preserve educational capacity and quality, to support "breeder centers" of international expertise. As the GAO has noted, "One cannot place a value on this apparatus, but if it is lost, it can be replaced in the future only at great cost over a long period of time" (U.S. GAO, 1978b, pp. 28-29). Basing support only on a market model could erode the system's capacity for research and its ability to produce needed specialists. The United States' involvement in Vietnam is commonly cited as an example of this dilemma: Employment demand failed to produce the experts on Vietnam who could have guided the nation away from that disastrous involvement. Another, related aspect of this problem—one that market forces also fail to solve—is how to "bank" international area specialists and revitalize them often enough to maintain their expertise.

Another shortcoming of a market model based on student demand for advanced international and area studies is that it cannot be relied upon to produce the requisite number of trained people. Because of the greater cost of teaching exotic languages, subjecting such programs to normal calculations of full-time equivalent (FTE) students would deter and probably diminish offerings of those languages. As Lambert (1978, p. 6) has observed, "It is absurd to have to justify support for a specialist in the Telegu language on the basis of the number of students he is training to be like him. There is not likely to be a great demand for these students if he does train them, but the nation has a stake in having one or two such specialists around."

While support for international studies should not be based solely on projections of employment demand for graduates, certainly such projections should be taken into account. Decisions on the appropriate level of support should look ahead rather than relating future need to past levels of support. Moreover, while it may not be possible to state precisely how much attention to advanced international and area studies is enough, the question of how much is *not* enough may be more answerable. For example, U.N. organizations are reluctant to hire Americans because they lack international experience! A GAO study of this situation noted that American candidates may be experts in their specialties, but all or most of their experience has been within the United States; they have not dealt much with different cultures, languages, educational systems, and political philosophies (U.S. GAO, 1977a, p. 20).

The percentage of students receiving M.A.'s at NDEA centers in the 1970s was two to three times the percentage receiving Ph.D.'s. Until 1977 (more recent data are not available), 40 to 50 percent of the M.A.'s continued their studies and 50 to 60 percent of the Ph.D.'s found jobs in higher education. Over 600 Ph.D.'s were produced annually by Title VI centers between 1973 and 1977; however, this figure has probably decreased. Recent trends suggest greater emphasis on the M.A., either as a terminal degree or followed by advanced work in a professional school. Although the employment prospects for M.A.'s have deteriorated somewhat, they may be better than those for Ph.D.'s. The success of M.A.'s from the general schools of international affairs (such as Georgetown's School of Foreign Service and the Fletcher School of Law and Diplomacy) in obtaining jobs in government or business, with the help of the vigorous placement programs of these institutions, reflects the much greater occupational orientation of this handful of institutions. It is also notable that their M.A.'s outnumber their Ph.D.'s by 8 or 10 to 1, in contrast to the ratio of 2 or 3 to 1 at area centers. This brings us to the demand for international-studies Ph.D.'s in higher education, government, and business.

The percentage of Ph.D.'s specializing in area studies at Title VI centers who obtained positions in higher education declined from 68.4 percent in 1970-71 to 54.6 percent in 1976-77. More recent figures are not available, but it is generally agreed that, because of the sharp decrease in outside funding, job opportunities in higher education for area specialists (as in a number of humanities and social-science fields) have diminished considerably. There is reason to be relatively optimistic about the prospects for retaining the present level of international-area-studies expertise at the major research universities—that is, replacing present faculty as they move or retire. There is a substantial cadre of tenured faculty committed to this goal at such universities, even though the present high percentage of tenured faculty implies few openings in the near future.

At other universities offering graduate work in international-area studies, the limited information available reveals an uneven picture. Most of the Ph.D.'s employed in higher education who are not at the major research universities are probably teaching at these institutions. An impressive amount of advanced training in area and international studies is being conducted at these institutions, even when there is no formal campus structure to focus and support it. Many of the faculty members are among the best in the country, as are the graduate students. Terminal or thesis master's programs are vigorous and varied, with increasing cooperation between international and area studies and professional schools—more so at the land-grant and state universities than at the major research universities—and with other institutions through consortial arrangements.

But impressive and useful as the graduate-level international programs of these second-tier institutions are, many face an uncertain future. In view of shrinking enrollments and diminishing financial support in both relative and absolute terms, these graduate programs will have difficulty holding their own, and those that undergo a critical erosion of resources may have trouble surviving at all. Few programs are likely to expand under present conditions. The net effect is a further decline in job opportunities in higher education for international and area studies graduates who lack advanced degrees from professional schools. Graduate enrollments in the second-tier institutions are responding more to this decline than enrollments at the major research universities. It is possible, of course, that this situation will change as a result of increased awareness of the need to strengthen international studies at all levels of the educational system.

The demand of the federal government for foreign-language, international, and area specialists is controversial. On the one hand, current staff recruitment patterns suggest no significant future increase; on the other hand, shortly after the president's commission came into being in October 1978, the Department of State and other agencies in the foreign-affairs establishment voiced deep concern over the inadequacies of the present system of advanced international-studies training. Although the relevant agencies need to recruit only a "thin stream" of highly trained people, a continuous output of such specialists is, in the view of these agencies, vital to the national interest. A perceived decline in the quality of specialists is a matter of concern, particularly as it applies to individuals who combine foreign-language and foreign-area expertise with at least one other discipline, rather than having area and language expertise only. Also disturbing to these agencies is the apparently diminished analytical ability of the international- and area-studies graduates recruited by foreign-affairs agencies, even in the current "buyer's market."

Notwithstanding these concerns, the federal government's demand for such people is unlikely to grow appreciably unless it becomes a policy for more government positions to be filled with these specialists, especially those with foreign-language skills. To take the Department of State as an example, its compliance rate in filling the 1,200 so-called foreign-language-designated positions in the Foreign Service with people who have the requisite language skills is relatively high (around 70 percent overall but only 40 percent in some key languages, especially Arabic and Korean). The needs of the Foreign Service for foreign-language and international-studies expertise now provide employment opportunities to few university graduates and, thus, minimal incentives for students to study or universities to offer advanced foreign-language and international studies; such incentives are further undermined by the absence of any foreign-language requirement for entry into the Foreign Service.

Under current circumstances, the essential issue is not the compliance rate of federal agencies but, for example, how many Foreign Service positions at what levels and in what specialties (political, commercial, consular, secretarial, and so on) should be defined as requiring those qualifications. Recently in a foreign capital, it was revealed that all the embassies of English-speaking countries, including that of the United States, depended for daily translations of the local press on an embassy wife who was a national of the country in question. The question of how many foreign-language positions are needed in American overseas posts thus certainly seems to call for a re-evaluation. A comparative study of how other countries, such as Japan and the Federal Republic of Germany, handle this matter might be illuminating.

If the defined needs of the federal bureaucracy corresponded to what the international relations of the United States require, government demand for foreign-language and international- and area-studies specialists might at least double, thereby strengthening the employment prospects of graduates in government and, through the multiplier effect, in the universities (to meet the resultant increased teaching demand). Another "Sputnik" incident may be required to catalyze such a decision; perhaps the ouster of the shah and subsequent developments in Iran should be recognized as such an event.

The needs and interests of the business community in foreign-language and international-studies expertise have an "Alice in Wonderland" quality. In the 1970s, the United States has lost much of its competitive advantage in world markets as technological advances in other countries, especially Japan and the Federal Republic of Germany, have caught up with and in some cases outstripped U.S. capabilities. If the balance-of-payments deficit is to be reduced, the United States must increase its exports, a goal to which the Carter administration is committed. While American exports have continued to rise in the past decade, the U.S. share of world exports has declined. The success of American business in gaining a significant portion of world trade with the People's Republic of China, now that diplomatic relations between it and the United States have been normalized, is far from assured; nor can one count on significant increases in U.S. trade with the Soviet Union (around $3 billion in 1978), even if the current U.S. restrictions on such trade, which make lower tariffs and export credits dependent on Soviet relaxation of emigration restrictions, cease to apply. If the United States is to compete successfully in these expanding markets, American business must become more sensitive to and knowledgeable about other countries and cultures and their languages. This need was emphasized in relation to the developing countries by an official of the World Bank: "Many of the problems of development aid and commerce are due to insufficient knowledge about the situation in the client country. Political, social, and cultural constraints have often been underestimated by foreign visitors. Lack of knowledge of the national languages has often restricted the visitors' communication to those groups in the community, which because of their upbringing may no longer have been representative of the society and therefore are unable to convey comprehensive information."[1]

Generalizations about the needs of business for foreign-language and international expertise are often rhetorical, misleading, or both. American multinational corporations engaged in exploiting the natural resources of other nations require greater appreciation of the cultural values of the countries where they operate than firms that are involved in developing the technology of another country, because the foreign country presumably is more interested in the latter. The larger American corporations, consulting firms with overseas clients, and banks have become increasingly aware of the importance of international expertise to their overseas operations. (The 13 largest American banks now derive about 50 percent of their total earnings from overseas operations.) This is especially true of firms whose activities require continual contact with people in the foreign country, a knowledge of local law affecting business and investment (for example Shari'a—the Islamic sacred or canon law—in the Arab world and beyond), and the framework within which the foreign economy operates (for example, five-year plans in the Soviet Union). In the past five to ten years, major American firms that are active internationally have increasingly tended to develop political-risk or political-assessment staffs to evaluate the noneconomic environment of countries in which they operate: These people forecast political and other developments that are likely to affect business and in general keep management informed on the foreign country's national concerns and plans.

In view of these conditions, there is likely to be almost no increase in the demand of American business for the graduates of advanced training programs in foreign languages and international studies. The major firms with political-assessment staffs virtually never hire recent graduates but typically select such individuals from within, a system that ensures the staffs a hear-

[1]M. Hultin to Ms. Graeme Baxter, Assistant Commissioner for Executive Operations, Office of Education (on the establishment of the President's Commission on Foreign Language and International Studies), August 30, 1977.

ing by their top management. In a few cases they recruit former Foreign Service officers. American businesses generally look for people with a technical background in marketing, finance, and the like, not with advanced training in a foreign language, area studies, or cross-cultural communication. Corporations operating abroad want people with this academic background, but only if it augments professional training in business or other fields. They will recruit business-school graduates and give them special training in foreign languages and area studies, but they almost never recruit foreign-language and area specialists and then give them special training in business. The priorities governing the recruitment of new personnel tend to be technical skills, adaptability, overseas experience, and foreign-language proficiency, in that order.

Although foreign-language and area studies Ph.D.'s are not likely to be hired by American businesses operating abroad, this is not the case with graduates of the general schools of international affairs, such as Georgetown's School of Foreign Service, the Johns Hopkins School of Advanced International Studies, and the Fletcher School of Law and Diplomacy. For some time, these schools have provided broad professional training. Their programs equip students, most of whom complete only an M.A., to deal with foreign governments and corporations and with international organizations through a combined program of international law and organization, economics and business relations, comparative politics, and area and cross-cultural studies offered on an interdisciplinary basis concurrently with foreign-language study. The flexibility of these graduate schools in adapting their curricula to the changing content of foreign affairs helps ensure that their graduates' training meets the functional needs of business and government.

In the long run, the most effective approach to strengthening the international expertise of American business would probably be to provide international training to business-school students. This involves building into the curricula of these schools courses that focus on international studies and the international aspects of business. An effort in this direction was mandated by a new accreditation requirement of the American

Assembly of Collegiate Schools of Business that the curricula of business schools include an international component. The requirement is so general, however, that its effectiveness is limited.

A major survey of business-school graduates, conducted in 1977, showed that some 75 percent of recent Ph.D.'s and D.B.A.'s had taken no international courses and that another 10 percent had taken only one international course (Nehrt, 1977). Few business-school faculty have international expertise, and the schools have few incentives to include internationally oriented courses in their offerings. Indeed, burgeoning business-school enrollments make it increasingly difficult to handle even standard curricula. This pressure also makes the schools reluctant to let students majoring in other fields enroll in their already overcrowded courses. Yet another deterrent is the fact that the business community does not encourage schools of business administration to internationalize their curricula.

However, the situation is not quite as bleak as the foregoing description suggests. Although recent data are not available, many students whose undergraduate work included international and area studies are enrolling in business schools for graduate work, thereby contributing to the internationalization of the student body, graduates, and eventually the staff recruited by American business. A parallel and more significant trend suggests that increasing numbers of graduate students in international and area studies earn a master's degree in this field and then pursue a graduate degree in business or in other professional fields, including law, health, and agriculture. The international- and area-studies centers and programs are beginning to encourage their students in this direction. Integrated or combined graduate degrees have also been developed at a few universities.

The needs of American business for staff with international expertise is likely to remain limited in terms of the numbers required for work abroad. Among the reasons are pressure to hire local rather than foreign staff, the increasing reliance of U.S. businesses on foreigners trained in this country, the high cost of supporting Americans in other countries, and the relatively short periods for which American staff are assigned abroad. However, if and when more small and middle-level American business firms become involved in international activities (only a tiny fraction of all American firms now export goods abroad; 100 firms account for half of total exports), international expertise will need to be dispersed more widely. The growing number of foreign firms investing in or setting up marketing and manufacturing branches in the United States is adding to this need.

At a broader level, just as it is in the interest of the federal government, so it is in the interest of business for Americans to have a more sophisticated appreciation of how the world works, greater sensitivity to cultural differences, and an understanding of the contribution of international trade to the national interest. Increased public awareness is essential to the "deprovincialization" of American business. The question of how much Title VI programs should contribute to such public awareness raises questions that are central to Title VI as a whole—namely, what functions international- and area-studies centers and programs should perform in the future, how these functions can be implemented, and what level of support they require.

Future Directions

For reasons mentioned earlier, it would not be appropriate for me to make detailed recommendations on advanced training and research in foreign-language and international and area studies. However, there is considerable support for the following general hypotheses:

1. A network of first-rate international- and area-studies centers is needed; this requires substantial federal support in order to (a) train faculty and researchers for the higher-education system, (b) produce the "thin stream" of highly qualified specialists required by federal agencies concerned with international affairs, and (c) provide international expertise for business and other professions involved in international activities.
2. The nation's international research needs, both inside and

outside of government, mandate the continuing support of a number of high-quality centers so that new information and ideas about other countries and international issues can be generated on a sustained basis, not as a shifting response to the foreign-policy preoccupations of the moment. The American centers abroad that facilitate international research require more predictable support than has been available to them in recent years.

3. The outstanding area-studies centers that now exist should serve as a national resource so that existing specialists, wherever they are, can revitalize and enhance their competence through postdoctoral research and related activities at these centers.

4. The center network should encompass all countries and their languages. It should also include comparative studies on problems of worldwide interest, such as revolutions and industrialization, because of the special value of examining these problems from a comparative perspective.

5. Related to the preceding function—and meriting greater priority—are (a) intercenter cooperation on problems spanning two or more major regions of the world and (b) collaboration between centers and professional schools. The tendency for area centers to be sealed off from other units on the same campus often impedes the development of joint programs and degrees, even though graduates of such programs have better job prospects than people with area specialization only.

6. In addition to the system of first-rate centers serving as a national resource, a regional network of second-tier centers and programs should be dispersed throughout the country. These regional centers should help strengthen international studies at all levels. Their outreach programs should include undergraduates within their own institutions as well as a range of organizations in the wider community, especially schools, adult-education groups, and other higher-education institutions in the region.

7. In keeping with the fact that much of the research on other countries and cultures is now carried out by scholars from

those countries, international- and area-studies centers in the United States should build bridges to centers in other countries through scholarly exchange and cooperative research.

All of these proposed functions and activities are being carried out to some extent both with and without NDEA Title VI funding. The basic questions, of course, are how much of what kinds of activities and programs should be supported in the future, and by whom. The high cost of maintaining first-rate centers requires rigorous selection among those aspiring to that status. The fact that employment opportunities for area-studies Ph.D.'s have diminished also suggests the imposition of some limits. In the context of these and other constraints, national needs for international and area studies should be analyzed in terms of a spectrum of functions at different levels, and a coherent long-range plan should be developed to meet these needs.

Debate on federal support for international- and area-studies centers and programs has suffered from a polarization of attitudes between those urging major long-term funding for relatively few centers and those favoring wider dispersion, both geographically and among institutions, of more limited support for limited periods—"to stimulate and encourage those who, at any given moment, do *not* have USOE money as well as those who do."[2] Also part of the debate is the priority that should be given to outreach programs, cooperation with professional schools, and undergraduate and terminal M.A. students in center programs, and the appropriate balance among area studies, professional international studies, and topical or problem-oriented studies.

The President's Commission on Foreign Language and International Studies faces a complex task in sorting out these issues and priorities. Among its concerns will be the system for making policy decisions relating to NDEA Title VI and how the concerns of foreign-affairs agencies, business and commerce, and other international interests might be represented in this process.

[2]P. T. Fisher, Jr., to Robert E. Ward, October 31, 1977.

We cannot ignore the fact that the anticipated demand on the part of higher education, government, and business for specialists in international and area studies is not expected to increase and may even diminish in the coming decade. But this fact should not be allowed to determine the appropriate level of federal and other funding for the field. Some comfort may be derived from the fact that the situation in the United States is not unique. An inquiry into area studies in Great Britain (Walker, 1977, p. 4) revealed a similar "lack of employer interest in area-studies graduates" and concern for area-studies funding even in the face of inadequate knowledge in that country about other parts of the world.

The employment situation for area-studies Ph.D.'s in the United States may require greater emphasis on postdoctoral support, professional-school programs (including professional international studies), and terminal M.A.'s. But a basic core of training and research must be maintained irrespective of the employment prospects of graduates and of the immediate relevance and applicability of the research. This was well articulated by Denis Sinor, Distinguished Professor of Uralic-Altaic Studies at Indiana University: "Just as it takes much obscure abstract research to produce a simple drug which may have a healing effect, it takes much obscure research to produce the knowledge and the body of experts capable of providing American leaders and educators with the information and knowledge needed to have an effective foreign policy and a favorable balance of payment."[3]

In short, market demand for people trained in international and area studies is only one of a number of pertinent considerations. If the demand does not assure these people of employment, it may be that the factors affecting the demand, rather than the supply, need alteration. Market demand should increase to correspond to the actual needs of the United States for international expertise in coping with a complex, increasingly interrelated world. To this end, public understanding of these needs should be enhanced, and the centers for advanced training and research should play an active role in this effort.

[3]Denis Sinor to Barbara B. Burn, May 24, 1979.

10

Organizing for
International
Education

The Present Situation

In calling for a more systematic approach to Harvard's international activities, President Derek Bok urged that "our separate activities relate to one another in a way that will make a whole that is greater than the sum of its parts" (1977, p. 34). Behind his statement is the notion that all of a university's activities should contribute to its larger purposes. With respect to international activities and programs, it has long been asserted that when such activities are centrally coordinated, they reinforce each other and become more central to the institution in terms of both structure and priority.

Efforts in this direction have increased over the years. When the International Education Act of 1966 was on the verge of passage, numerous colleges and universities set up international program offices to implement this legislation. The number of such offices increased from 12 in 1964 to 186 in 1969 and an estimated 832 (probably high) in 1974 (Sanders and Ward, 1970). Typically, they grew out of the institution's foreign-student offices (like those of Texas, Michigan, and Cornell). A 1977 survey (Committee for International Studies and Programs Administrators [CISPA], 1978) indicated that, of 336 responding institutions, only 29 had staffs whose job was to coordinate international-studies activities, including those of both academic and service divisions.

Ralph H. Smuckler, Dean of International Studies and Programs at Michigan State University (which, incidentally, is one of the few American universities that effectively centralizes international programs at a high level), has described the structural arrangements for international studies as follows: [1]

> There is a polyglot of arrangements. In general, international-studies interests on American university campuses are organized rather weakly from the standpoint of asserting any institutional leverage. At only a few institutions does one find what might be considered political strength incorporated in the international program structure. Most of the universities reflect a combination of alliances among various "baronies," which are based on disciplinary and professional-school interests. The constituent parts of most international-program efforts, namely international-studies and area-study centers, are in general negotiating with these various alliances and baronies for resources and acknowledgment within the institution. Only rarely does the central international-studies center have direct access to the power centers of the university in the central administration. Furthermore, in most institutions, the central unit for international-programs activity is not broadly inclusive, frequently omitting AID contractual efforts or foreign student affairs and/or area studies. The typical international-programs organization is made up of rather politically weak individuals who do not think strategically about the interrelated goals or segments of the international programs and, therefore, are easily bypassed or largely ineffective in their attempts to influence institutional policy. Therein lies one of the basic difficulties in moving toward a strong inter-

[1] Ralph H. Smuckler to Barbara B. Burn, July 18, 1977.

national dimension within our various institutions, or nationally.

In a 1977 study of international education in the California State University and Colleges, the chief obstacles limiting the development of an international education program were identified as "first, the lack of a comprehensive international-education policy and, secondly, the lack of administrative offices to coordinate the various facets of international education at the CSUC system and local campus level" (Knudson, 1977, pp. 10-11). A similar point was made in a 1971 study of interinstitutional cooperation in international education among 34 colleges and universities in Ohio, West Virginia, and Pennsylvania. It found that the effectiveness of international programs depended on support by the institution's top administrative leadership and on faculty receptivity (Hoopes and others, 1971).

An important objective of the Ford Foundation's international training and research program was to encourage international education programs "to grow institutional sinews that could overcome or counterbalance the powerful centripetal force of the traditional discipline" (Ford Foundation, 1978). In its negotiations with universities, the foundation deliberately asked that they make their proposals in the context of their overall interests and plans. As a consequence, the universities were impelled to set up planning bodies that included representatives of all the various faculties and colleges as well as top administrators; institutions that did not receive Ford Foundation grants were stimulated to develop committees on international programs and planning. The growth of AID-supported university contracts and Peace Corps training programs after 1961 greatly increased the need for universitywide review of international activities and for expanded staffing of such activities.

OE deserves considerable credit for strengthening the commitment of American colleges and universities to international studies. Through its programs, it has encouraged linkages among various disciplines and between international-studies programs and the professional schools. The inclusion of a variety of exchange activities among the criteria for the selection of Title VI area centers encourages institutions to provide overseas experience for faculty and students and to cooperate with foreign scholars, institutions, and governments. Center funding criteria also include "the extent to which cooperative arrangements have been worked out with other departments, schools, and special and professional programs of the grantee institution and the extent to which the center includes appropriate multi- and inter-disciplinary instruction" (*Federal Register,* 1977, p. 26210).

As mentioned in Chapter 7, AID grants under Title XII of the Foreign Assistance Act of 1975 also provide incentive to universities, mainly land- and sea-grant institutions, to increase their international commitments—in this case to economic development. To qualify for strengthening grants, eligible institutions must meet certain criteria regarding institutional commitment—for example, the extent to which promotion and tenure policies reward faculty work abroad. A major requirement for these matching grants is that the university invest its own funds in improving its development assistance capacity.

Problems and Possible Solutions

The decentralized departmental and faculty structure of universities and colleges, always an obstacle to intrainstitutional coordination, is probably becoming more rigid. Not only do financial pressures limit faculty promotions and new appointments, but departments that are trying to keep up their FTEs are increasingly reluctant to let their members take on extradepartmental teaching. Steven Muller, President of Johns Hopkins University, has commented on this tendency toward departmentalism as follows (1978, p. 2): "Much of the world in which a typical faculty member operates daily is bounded by his or her academic department. Such circumstances do not encourage interdisciplinary work among faculty. Aside from the difficulties of bridging fields that engage scholars in this age of extreme specialization, work that is interdisciplinary is also interdepartmental. This often adds organizational obstacles to substantive problems. . . . To succeed, [interdisciplinary] work must overcome the built-in resistance created by the autonomous department."

In addition to facing the obstacle of departmentalism, universitywide coordination of international programs must deal with the likelihood of competition among the programs themselves. Appeals for coordination of study-abroad programs and foreign-student activities tend to ignore the fact that most of the American students who study abroad go to Western Europe, but most of the foreign students in the United States are from the developing countries. Area-studies faculty, who are mainly in the humanities and social sciences, have little in common with the agricultural, engineering, and other professional faculty who are active in development assistance. This situation is changing, however, and greater coordination may emerge as development assistance gives more emphasis to cooperation between the professions and the social sciences.

The competitiveness just described is supported by Lambert's observation (1973, p. 276) that different kinds of international programs do not flourish equally at any given campus; instead, one kind usually dominates. Lambert also found that the growth of strong area-studies programs seems to be inhibited by the existence of other kinds of international programs, including a "highly centralized and well-funded administration for international studies." Does this mean that one set of interests prospers at the expense of others, as Lambert suggests? Or does the launching of one program foster the emergence of others in its wake? The case studies needed to answer these questions have not been undertaken. Indeed, it is regrettable that the Ford Foundation, which has actively encouraged universitywide mechanisms to coordinate and strengthen international programs, has not yet analyzed the impact of these efforts.

If a central administrative office or committee for international studies and programs is only an advisory unit (which is usually the case), the strength of an international program is likely to reflect its ability to obtain outside funding rather than the priorities of the central administrative unit. A major factor that could impede the integration of various kinds of international programs is the attitude of the scholars and academic entrepreneurs who built up major programs and centers, especially in the 1960s, and may not want their authority diminished by a central office or committee. But even when a central unit has decision-making authority, only rarely will it have a significant impact on the relative growth rates of different programs. In committees that represent competing international interests, members are loath to reject proposals from one interest group lest at a later date their own proposals are rejected by vengeful colleagues. An international-programs office is under comparable pressure to placate competing groups. Under the circumstances, it is not surprising that a university's international involvements tend to grow at their own speed and that the more developed ones retain their edge over the others, thus confirming Lambert's observations.

Despite these difficulties, it is more important than ever that coordination of international programs be attempted. Those involved in area studies, technical assistance, and other international activities should collaborate more closely for reasons of both survival and impact. Working alone, each is vulnerable to budget cutting and has a limited constituency to defend it when the pressure is on. Working together, they can make international studies and programs more central to the institution, enlarge their constituency, and enrich and extend their contributions.

In the preceding chapters, I have suggested various ways in which institutions can strengthen their international education programs. These include the following:

1. Using foreign students as a teaching resource.
2. Involving faculty with experience in development assistance in international-studies programs (for example, as guest lecturers in African-studies courses).
3. Using experts in international studies for the predeparture orientation of faculty who are about to participate in development-assistance programs.
4. Increasing the collaboration between international education programs and professional schools, with the twofold goal of

internationalizing curricula in the latter and encouraging area-studies majors to obtain professional as well as international training.
5. Finding ways of incorporating overseas experience into academic counseling.
6. Making greater use of international-studies faculty and graduate students to develop links with institutions of higher education in appropriate regions.

Cumulatively, these efforts can result in the integration of international education into a college or university in such a way that, in Bok's words, the whole will be greater than the sum of its parts.

Progress to Date

At the regional and national levels, American higher education is far better organized for international studies than it was a decade ago. Regional consortia and collaborative programs to exchange information, pool resources, and coordinate programs have multiplied, but with varying degrees of effectiveness. In the field of Soviet and East European studies, for example, there are now about eight arrangements of this sort. Title VI area centers are explicitly encouraged to cooperate with other institutions. The Midwest Universities Consortium for International Activities provides a structure for collaboration among seven major state universities; members of the Great Lakes Colleges Association and the Associated Colleges of the Mid-West also coordinate their study-abroad programs. In Massachusetts, the Statewide Committee for International Programs was relatively effective for several years in the mid-1970s in facilitating cooperation in international education, mainly through information sharing, among the public-sector institutions in that state. However, it eventually succumbed to the pressures of budget limits, inertia, and shifting priorities.

The constraints of geography, funds, institutional support, and faculty time remain significant deterrents to effective cooperation in international education. However, interinstitutional competition may be diminishing as pressures on higher education in general spur greater cooperation. The experiences of consortia and collaborative programs focusing on one major region—the Soviet Union and Eastern Europe—reveal some of the problems involved in achieving effective collaboration (Jones, 1977, p. 2): "Cooperative programs worked best when cooperation at the highest administrative levels had been worked out between the separate institutions from the top down before the faculties at the individual institutions began their own cooperative efforts, when there was a financial reason or necessity for such cooperation, and where the distances were not so great as to impede cooperation."

At the national level, the organization of international studies is much stronger than it was even five years ago. The International Education Project (IEP) of the American Council on Education (ACE), established in August 1973, has played a critical role in rallying support for the funding of Title VI. The studies of the current state of international education conducted by six task forces coordinated by IEP's Interface Committee provided an extremely useful review and assessment (ACE, 1975a). ACE's decision in June 1978 to replace the IEP with a new Division of International Educational Relations, along with a new commission, may result in even more active representation of the international interests of higher education.

The other national higher-education associations are also active in international education. The International Programs and Studies Office of the National Association of State Universities and Land-Grant Colleges (NASULC) vigorously supports the international interests of its member institutions, especially with respect to the Department of Agriculture, the Agency for International Development (AID), the Board for International Food and Agricultural Development (BIFAD), and the proposed Institute for Scientific and Technological Cooperation (ISTC). The international office and staff of the American Association of Colleges for Teacher Education (AACTE), in existence since the early 1970s, promotes international education in teaching training institutions. Both the American Association of Community and Junior Colleges (AACJC) and the American Association of State Colleges and Universities (AASCU) have an increasingly strong interest in international education and actively represent their members' interests before Congress, federal agencies, and the foundations. In addition, although the priorities of the various associations just mentioned differ because of the differences in their constituencies and the basic pluralism of American higher education, they often engage in consultation on matters related to international education.

Conclusions

The pluralism and complexity of higher education in the United States can be bewildering to people in other countries. It also means that there is no single voice speaking for American higher education to institutions and agencies abroad. While the International Communication Agency (ICA) represents the United States on matters of cultural and educational policy, the existence of the federal system in the United States makes it impossible for federal agencies, including ICA, to claim to represent the American higher education system vis-à-vis other countries. The disarray of American higher education in dealing with the People's Republic of China on scholarly exchanges—which was characterized by competition among the universities, the higher-education professional associations, and even federal agencies— amply demonstrates the decentralization of American higher education.

The absence of an American agency comparable to the ministries of higher education found in other countries is sometimes viewed as an impediment to the development of international educational exchanges and other international arrangements. However, the fact that American colleges and universities can initiate such arrangements without having to go through a ministry of education affords them much more flexibility than is possible in countries with more centralized systems. The proposed establishment of a separate Department of Education in the federal government is not likely to alter this situation because of the lack of federal jurisdiction over education in the United States.

As mentioned earlier, to facilitate communication and linkages between American and foreign institutions, six major associations agreed in 1976 to sponsor a study of international linkages in higher education (Harrington, 1978). Its purpose was to explore ways in which American colleges and universities could increase their effectiveness in dealing with higher-education institutions abroad, emphasizing not only the developing world but the middle-income nations and the developed world as well. The draft of its report recommended the establishment of a Council for International Cooperation in Higher Education (CICHE), but this organization never saw the light of day. Nonetheless, there appears to be consensus that the CICHE proposal had some merit. The need for a clearinghouse for communication between higher-education institutions in the United States and abroad remains strong. Such an organization would facilitate interinstitutional contacts, attempt to meet the information needs of foreign agencies and organizations seeking to place students in U.S. colleges and universities, and facilitate access by foreign institutions to the appropriate U.S. institutions for purposes of technical assistance, program development, collaborative research, staff development, and the like.

In view of the new responsibility of ICA to coordinate all the educational exchanges of the federal government, as well as its continuing role in international educational policy, assigning the clearinghouse function to ICA is a possible solution. If a new Department of Education is established and brings together the international-education programs currently supervised by OE and other agencies, the exchange clearinghouse might be located in the new department.

Much activity along these lines already takes place—for example, through the Fulbright program, through the activities of the Institute for International Education in recruiting and placing American scholars in institutions abroad, as part of AID programs, to a very limited extent by NDEA Title VI centers, as part of the activities of universities receiving BIFAD strengthening grants, and under other auspices. The ISTC, if it comes into being, will be important in encouraging interinstitutional linkages, especially between U.S. and developing-country universities. A cooperative arrangement among some of the professional associations in higher education, known as the Global Education Group,[2] has as one of its functions the provision of "a central contact point for those wishing access to higher education, both within and without the U.S." (Global Education Group, n.d.).

It has been suggested that an expanded clearinghouse to facilitate cooperation between American and foreign higher-education institutions should be established either within ICA or within the new Department of Education. However, in the view of more experienced observers, a unit serving both the clearinghouse and linkage functions should be set up outside of the federal government. The Overseas Liaison Committee of the American Council on Education, which for some time has carried out such functions in relation to higher education in Africa and the Caribbean, offers one approach. Its work, which is much better known and more respected abroad than in the United States, has become even more important as a result of Nigeria's recent interest in sending large numbers of students to the United States.

Another useful model is the Overseas Education Service (OES), which was set up in association with Education and World Affairs, largely with Carnegie Corporation support, and functioned for about eight years in the 1960s. OES identified the needs of universities in developing countries for faculty with specific disciplinary expertise, recruited American faculty to fill those positions, and provided them with salary supplements at reasonable levels. The genius of the OES was its highly individualized approach, its relatively low cost, and the opportunities it made available to Americans from a wide range of institutions without the complexities of expensive large-scale university contracts. In keeping with changes in the international community and the greater importance of reciprocity in relations between the United States and third-world countries, a new OES emphasizing two-way exchanges could make

[2]Member organizations are the American Association of Colleges for Teacher Education, the American Association of Community and Junior Colleges, and American Association of State Colleges and Universities, the International Council on Education for Teaching, and the National Association of State Universities and Land Grant Colleges.

a contribution to internationalizing American higher education.

The 1980s are likely to offer more opportunities for cooperation by American higher-education institutions with their counterparts abroad as well as more deterrents to such cooperation. Interdependence, the greater need to learn from and about others, the increasing mobility of people throughout the world, the global nature of many problems and their solutions, and the expansion of higher-education systems in the developing world —all of these factors will give impetus to cooperation between universities in the United States and other countries. Significant in this context is the number of people from other countries who come to the United States for their higher education and return home to staff their own colleges and universities. Many retain or revive their ties with their American alma maters and look to the United States for scholarly communication and interchange. The increasing debate on North-South relations, together with developing-country demands for cooperation on the basis of reciprocity, lends added force to this trend. In this connection, it is noteworthy that the ISTC, one potential American response to these demands, may involve nationals from other countries in its functioning even though it is an instrument of the U.S. government.

The deterrents to cooperation between American colleges and universities and higher-education institutions abroad may loom larger than the needs and opportunities for such cooperation. Pressure on financial resources, often translated into a need to give priority to local, regional, and national needs at the cost of international priorities, is a worldwide phenomenon to which American higher education is daily more vulnerable, especially in the public sector. These financial pressures appear to be bringing into the management of American institutions, at least the major state universities, a breed of administrators who are more attuned to PPBS than to forging links with intellectuals in other nations. Also, the growing demands for public accountability, which are eroding the autonomy of higher-education systems everywhere, may make American universities less able to reach out to universities abroad—less free to engage in activi-

ties whose payoff is not readily quantifiable into tangible benefits for local taxpayers. International cooperation is singularly
vulnerable in this respect.

The future offers mixed promises. While much is happen-
ing in international education, it falls far short of national
needs. In its comprehensive sense, international education
should be considered an integral part of the responsibilities and
involvements of the United States. It should be an important
part of the activities and structure of American colleges and universities and of professional associations and governmental agencies concerned with higher education. The pluralism and diversity of the American scene have made possible a variety of
initiatives, and it is true that this situation offers many advantages. But unless international education is raised to the level of
a national commitment, it will continue to be peripheral to
many colleges and universities and will be a victim of competition at the campus level and among national organizations. For
international education to become a major priority enlisting
coordinated support at all levels, institutional and national leadership must recognize and articulate this priority and match
rhetoric with resources.

References

Abrams, I. "The Impact of Antioch Education Through Experience Abroad." Paper presented at the annual meeting of the International Studies Association. Washington, D.C., Feb. 23, 1978.

Academy for Educational Development. *World Studies Data Bank Annual Report, 1974-75.* New York: 1975.

Alger, C. I. *People in the Future Global Order.* Report 22. Columbus, Ohio: Mershon Center, March 1978a.

Alger, C. I. "People in the Future Global Order." *Alternatives: A Journal of World Policy,* April 1978b, *4* (1).

Alger, C. I., and Hoover, D. C. *You and Your Community in the World.* Columbus, Ohio: Consortium for International Studies Education, Ohio State University, 1978.

Allen, H. B. "The Teaching of English as a Second Language and U.S. Foreign Policy." Address to the 12th annual convention of Teachers of English to Speakers of Other Languages (TESOL). Mexico City, April 5, 1978.

American Academy of Arts and Sciences. "The Purpose of Pugwash—Past and Future." *Bulletin of the American Academy of Arts and Sciences,* Feb. 1978, *31* (5).

American Council on Education, International Education Project. *Education for Global Interdependence.* Washington, D.C.: 1975a.

American Council on Education, Task Force on Library and Information Resources. *Library Resources for International Education.* Washington, D.C.: 1975b.

American Council on Education. *Task Force on Mid-Term Research for Foreign Policy: Final Report.* Washington, D.C.: 1977.

Arbeiter, S., and others. *40 Million Americans in Career Transition.* New York: College Entrance Examination Board, 1978.

Ashby, Sir E. *Any Person, Any Study: An Essay on American Higher Education.* Carnegie Commission on Higher Education. New York: McGraw-Hill, 1971.

Astin, A., King, M. R., and Richardson, G. T. *The American Freshman: National Norms for Fall 1977.* Los Angeles: Laboratory for Research in Higher Education, Graduate School of Education, University of California, Los Angeles, 1978.

Atelsek, F. J., and Gomberg, I. L. *Foreign Area Research Support Within Organized Research Centers at Selected Universities, Fiscal Years 1972 and 1976.* Higher Education Panel Reports 32. Washington, D.C.: American Council on Education, Dec. 1976.

Atelsek, F. J., and Gomberg, I. L. *Scientific and Technical Cooperation with Developing Countries, 1977-78.* Washington, D.C.: American Council on Education, 1978.

Auden, W. H. "Journey to Iceland." In *Letters from Iceland.* London: Faber & Faber, 1937.

Ben-David, J. *American Higher Education: Directions Old and New.* Carnegie Commission on Higher Education. New York: McGraw-Hill, 1972.

Blaug, M. *Bildungsökonomie und Entwicklungsländer: Gegenwärtige Trends und Neue Prioritäten* [Economics of education in developing countries: Current trends and new priorities]. Berlin: Max-Planck-Institut für Bildungsforschung, 1977.

Bloomfield, I. C. (Rapporteur). *Public Opinion and Foreign Policy in a Democracy.* Endicott House Workshop, May 21-22, 1976. Dayton, Ohio: Charles F. Kettering Foundation, June 15, 1976.

Board of Foreign Scholarships. *Reviewing the Commitment: Seventh Annual Report.* Washington, D.C.: 1969.

Board of Foreign Scholarships. *Report on Exchanges, December 1975: Thirteenth Annual Report.* Washington, D.C.: U.S. Government Printing Office, 1976.

Board of Foreign Scholarships. *Report on Exchanges.* Washington, D.C.: U.S. Government Printing Office, 1977.

Board for International Food and Agricultural Development. *Questions and Answers About University Participation in Title XII Programs.* Washington, D.C.: Aug. 28, 1977.

Bok, D. *President's Report 1975-76. Harvard University.* Cambridge, Mass.: Harvard University Publications Office, 1977.

Born, W. C., and Buck, C. (Compilers). *Options for the Teaching of Foreign Languages, Literatures, and Cultures.* New York: American Council on the Teaching of Foreign Languages, Inc., 1978.

Brod, R. I. *Survey of Foreign-Language Course Registrations in U.S. Colleges and Universities, Fall 1977.* Washington, D.C.: U.S. Department of Health, Education, and Welfare, Aug. 1978.

Brookings Institution. *An Assessment of Development Assistance Strategies.* Interim report. Washington, D.C.: Oct. 6, 1977.

Brown, L. *The Global Economic Prospect: New Sources of Economic Stress.* Washington, D.C.: Worldwatch Institute, 1978.

Buergenthal, T., and Torney, J. V. *International Human Rights and International Education.* Washington, D.C.: U.S. National Commission for UNESCO, 1976.

Burke, F. (New Jersey State Commissioner of Education). Presentation to the President's Commission on Foreign Language and International Studies. Transcript of proceedings, Vol. 2. Washington, D.C.: Oct. 26-27, 1978.

Burn, B. B. *Higher Education in Nine Countries: A Comparative Study of Colleges and Universities Abroad.* Carnegie Commission on Higher Education. New York: McGraw-Hill, 1971.

Burn, B. B. (Ed.). *Higher Education Reform: Implications for Foreign Students.* New York: Institute of International Education, 1978.

Callaghan, J. "More than the Market in Common." *New York Times,* June 30, 1978.

Cameron, J. "Arms and the Men." *Manchester Guardian Weekly,* June 4, 1978, *118* (23).

The Carnegie Foundation for the Advancement of Teaching. *Mission of the College Curriculum: A Contemporary Review with Suggestions.* San Francisco: Jossey-Bass, 1977.

Caroux, R. "Trends in Language and Cultural Studies." In S. K. Bailey (Ed.), *Higher Education in the World Community.* Washington, D.C.: American Council on Education, 1977.

Cellard, J. "L'Anglicisation de la Jeunesse Française" [The anglicizing of french youth]. *Le Monde de l'Education* [The world of education], April 1977, *27.*

Chittick, W. O. *The Group Perspective in Foreign Policy: A Report on U.S. World Affairs Organizations (NGOs).* Athens: University of Georgia Press, 1977.

Chyter, N. "Survey of 50 Community College Catalogs." A private study commissioned for B. B. Burn, July 1977.

Cleveland, H. *A Passion for Paradox.* New York: Global Perspectives in Education, 1977a.

Cleveland, H. *The Future of the Aspen Peace Corps.* Princeton, N.J.: Aspen Institute Program in International Affairs, 1977b.

Cleveland, H. "The Domestication of International Affairs and Vice Versa." *Annals of the American Academy of Political and Social Science,* March 1979, *442,* 125-137.

Clymer, A. "Poll Finds Public Looks on Peking More Favorably Than on Moscow." *New York Times,* Feb. 2, 1979.

College Entrance Examination Board, Admissions Testing Program. *College-Bound Seniors 1971-72.* New York: 1974.

College Entrance Examination Board, Admissions Testing Program. *National Report: College-Bound Seniors 1978.* New York: 1978a.

College Entrance Examination Board. *The Foreign Student in United States Community and Junior Colleges.* New York: 1978b.

College Entrance Examination Board. *Guidelines for the Recruitment of Foreign Students.* New York: 1978c.

Collins, H. T. *Global Education and the States: Some Observations, Some Programs, and Some Suggestions.* New York: American Field Service, 1977.

Committee on the College and World Affairs. *The College and World Affairs.* New York: The Hazen Foundation, 1964.

Committee for International Studies and Programs Administrators. "International Studies Survey Results." *CISPA Newsletter*, Jan. 1978, *1* (1), 2-3.

Committee on the University and World Affairs. (S. L. Morrill, Chairman.) *The University and World Affairs*. New York: Ford Foundation, 1960.

Coughlin, E. K. "Language Scholars Face Hard Choices in Ph.D. Training." *Chronicle of Higher Education*, Jan. 9, 1978a, *15* (17).

Coughlin, E. K. "Educators Seek to Broaden Liberal-Arts Goals." *Chronicle of Higher Education*, Feb. 21, 1978b, *15* (23).

Council of Chief State School Officers, Committee on International Education. *Civic Literacy for Global Interdependence: New Challenge to State Leadership in Education*. Washington, D.C.: 1976.

Council on International Educational Exchange. *Evaluating Academic Programs Abroad: The CIEE Project*. New York: 1978.

Council on Learning. *Education and the World View*. New Rochelle, N.Y.: 1977. (Mimeo.)

Derham, Sir D. *The Mobility of Students and Staff Internationally*. Twelfth Commonwealth Universities Congress. Vancouver: Association of Commonwealth Universities, Aug. 19-25, 1978.

Eason, W. W. "Prospectus and First Progress Report." Unpublished paper, American Association for the Advancement of Slavic Studies, Dynamic Inventory of Soviet and East European Studies in the United States. Columbus, Ohio, Oct. 1977.

Eason, W. W. "Report on the First Results." Unpublished paper, American Association for the Advancement of Slavic Studies, Dynamic Inventory of Soviet and East European Studies in the United States. Columbus, Ohio, Oct. 1978.

Ellison, H. "Changing Needs in Center Curricula." Presentation to the NDEA Center Directors' Meeting. Arlington, Va., Oct. 16, 1977.

Emerson, R. W. "The American Scholar." Phi Beta Kappa address delivered at Harvard University, 1839. In B. Atkinson (Ed.), *The Selected Writings of Ralph Waldo Emerson*. New York: Random House, 1940.

Federal Register, May 23, 1977, *42* (99).

"Final Enrollment Count Shows Total Up 2.6 Percent from 1976." *Higher Education and National Development*, June 23, 1978, *27* (14).

Ford Foundation. "Tight Market for College Teachers." *Ford Foundation Letter*, Feb. 1, 1977, *8* (1).

Ford Foundation. *Research Universities and the National Interest: A Report from Fifteen University Presidents*. New York: 1978.

Fox, M. J. *Language and Development: A Retrospective Survey of Ford Foundation Language Projects 1952-1954*. New York: Ford Foundation, 1975.

"The Geography of Languages Taught at U.S. Colleges." *Chronicle of Higher Education*, Aug. 7, 1978, *16* (22).

Gilligan, J. J. Quoted in "Gilligan: AID and Aid Under Attack." *The Independent*, Feb. 1978, *5* (2).

Global Education Group in U.S. Higher Education. Undated flyer. (Available from Global Education Group in U.S. Higher Education, One Dupont Circle, Washington, D.C.)

Gould, H. A. "Funding Prospects for South Asian Studies." Paper presented at the meeting of the South Asian Council of the Association for Asian Studies. Ann Arbor, Mich., Nov. 1979.

Grant, S. A. *Language Policy in the United States.* Washington, D.C.: Kennan Institute for Advanced Russian Studies, 1978. (Mimeo.)

Gray, A. W. *International/Intercultural Education in Selected State Colleges and Universities.* Washington, D.C.: American Association of State Colleges and Universities, 1977.

Great Britain, Minister of Education. "Education in Schools: A Consultative Document." Education Green Paper, 1977. In G. Fowler, "Revolution in Green." *Times Education Supplement* (London), Aug. 5, 1977.

Hafiz, T. (Program Director, Ministry of Higher Education, Saudi Arabian Educational Mission). "235,000 Foreign Students in U.S. Colleges and Universities: Impact and Response." Speech at a symposium organized by the National Association for Foreign Student Affairs. Center of Adult Education, University of Maryland, Sept. 25-26, 1978.

Hansen, J. S., and Gladieux, L. E. *Middle-Income Students: A New Target for Federal Aid?* New York: College Entrance Examination Board, 1978.

Hanvey, R. G. *An Attainable Global Perspective.* New York: Center for War/Peace Studies, 1976.

Harrington, F. H. (Director). *International Linkages in Higher Education: A Feasibility Study.* Preliminary report. Washington, D.C.: International Linkages in Higher Education, Feb. 1978.

Harvard University, Faculty of Arts and Sciences. *Report on the Core Curriculum.* Cambridge, Mass.: Harvard University Press, Feb. 15, 1978.

Hayden, R. L. "Internationalizing Public Education: What the States Are Doing." *International Educational and Cultural Exchange,* Fall 1976a, *12* (2).

Hayden, R. L. "Relating Language to International Education: Some Do's and Don't's." *ADFL Bulletin,* Nov. 1976b, *8* (2).

Hayden, R. L. Statement Before the Senate Appropriations Subcommittee on Labor/Department of Health, Education, and Welfare. Sept. 21, 1977.

Hayden, R. L. *A Rationale for International Education: Facing Facts.* Washington, D.C.: American Council on Education, International Education Project, n.d. (Mimeo.)

Higher Education and National Affairs, Jan. 20, 1978, *27* (3): 4.

Hoopes, D. S., and others. *A Study of the Dynamics of the Interinstitutional Cooperation for International Education Development.* Pittsburgh: Regional Council for International Education, 1971.

Hull, F., IV, Lemke, W. H., Jr., and Ting-ku Houang, R. *The American Undergraduate, Off-Campus and Overseas: A Study of the Educational Validity of Such Programs.* New York: Council on International Educational Exchange, 1977.

Husèn, T. "Evaluation Reflections, Policy Implications of the IEA Findings and Some of Their Repercussions on National Debates on Educational Policy." *Studies in Educational Evaluation*, Summer 1977, *3* (2), 137.

Institute of International Education. *Annual Report 1977*. New York: 1977a.

Institute of International Education. Translation of *Lettre d'Information* of the Office National des Universites et Ecoles Françaises, June 1977b.

International Communication Agency. "The Statement of Mission for the International Communication Agency transmitted by President Jimmy Carter to Ambassador John E. Reinhardt on March 13, 1978." *International Educational and Cultural Exchange*, Summer 1978, *14* (1).

Jenkins, H. M. "International Education and NAFSA, 1948-1978." *International Educational and Cultural Exchange*, Summer 1978, *14* (1).

Jones, R. E. Unpublished report prepared for B. B. Burn, Nov. 1977.

Julian, A. C., and Slattery, R. E. *Open Doors 1975/6-1976/7*. New York: Institute of International Education, 1978.

Kelleher, A. C. "A Report on the Status of International Studies Curricula in Massachusetts Community Colleges." Private study commissioned for B. B. Burn, Aug. 1977.

Kinghorn, J. R. "School Improvement Through Global Education." *North Central Association Quarterly*, Spring 1978, *52* (4): 449-454.

Kinghorn, J. R., and Shaw, W. F. *Handbook for Global Education: A Working Manual*. Dayton, Ohio: Charles F. Kettering Foundation, 1977.

Klassen, F. H., Imig, D. C., and Yff, J. *The International Dimension of American Teacher Education*. Washington, D.C.: American Association of Colleges for Teacher Education, 1973.

Knudsen, R. G. "A Fault Free Approach to an International Education Program: California State University and Colleges." Dissertation abstract, University of Southern California, April 1977.

Kulakow, A. M. *Foreign Policy Forums, Spring 1976*. Dayton, Ohio: Charles F. Kettering Foundation, May 7, 1976.

Lambert, R. D. *Language and Area Studies Review*. Philadelphia: American Academy of Political and Social Science, 1973.

Lambert, R. D. "A Frame of Reference for Federal Interest in International Studies." Statement submitted to the House Committee on International Relations, Subcommittee on International Operations, Oct. 3, 1978.

Levine, A. *Handbook on Undergraduate Curriculum: Prepared for the Carnegie Council on Policy Studies in Higher Education*. San Francisco: Jossey-Bass, 1978.

Luxemberg, S. "All the Class a Stage." *Change, Report on Teaching 5*, Jan. 1978, *10* (1).

McCaughey, R. A. "The Permanent Revolution: An Assessment of the Current State of International Studies in American Universities." Unpublished manuscript, Barnard College, Columbia University, Jan. 1979.

McDowell, E. "Foreign-Policy Buffs Hail 60 Years of Fighting Isolationism." *New York Times*, Feb. 2, 1978.

Magrath, C. P. (President, University of Minnesota). Panel presentation at annual meeting of the National Association of State Universities and Land-Grant Colleges. St. Louis, Mo., Nov. 13, 1978.

Mark Associates, Inc. *Eisenhower Exchange Fellowships, Inc., 1976 Fellows Survey*. Washington, D.C.: 1976.

Markovits, A. S., and Keeler, J. T. "The Euro-Consciousness of American College Students: A Survey of Knowledge and Attitudes at Five 'Elite' Institutions." *European Studies Newsletter*, May 1978, 7 (6).

Massey, E. T., and Massey, J. A. *CULCON Report on Japanese Studies at Colleges and Universities in the United States in the Mid-'70s*. Study prepared for the Subcommittee on Japanese Studies, American Panel, U.S.-Japan Conference on Cultural and Educational Interchange. New York: Japan Society, March 1977.

Mehlinger, H. *Descriptions of "Outreach Activities" of 45 Centers for Language and Area Studies*. Bloomington, Ind.: Social Studies Development Center, Indiana University, and Mid-America Center, Dec. 1976.

Mestenhauser, J. A., and Barsig, D. *Foreign Student Advisors and Learning with Foreign Students and Foreign Teachers*. Washington, D.C.: National Association for Foreign Student Affairs, n.d.

Modern Language Association. *Task Force on the Commonly Taught Languages: Draft Final Report*. New York: 1978a.

Modern Language Association. *Survey of Foreign Language Courses Registrations in U.S. Colleges and Universities, Fall 1977*. Washington, D.C.: U.S. Department of Health, Education, and Welfare, Office of Education, Division of International Education, August 1978b.

Modern Language Association. *A National Ten-Year Plan for Teaching and Training in the Less Commonly Taught Languages: Source Materials for the Report of the MLA/ACLS Task Force on the Less Commonly Taught Languages*. Final revision. New York: March 26, 1979.

Muller, S. "The President's Message." *Annual Report of the President*. Baltimore, Md.: Johns Hopkins University Publications Office, 1978.

Murthy, K. S. *Student and Staff Mobility Under Federalism*. Twelfth Commonwealth Universities Congress. Vancouver: Association of Commonwealth Universities, Aug. 19-25, 1978.

Nagai, M. *An Owl Before Dusk*. Berkeley: Carnegie Commission on Higher Education, 1975.

National Association for Foreign Student Affairs. *The Relevance of U.S. Graduate Programs to Foreign Students From Developing Countries*. Washington, D.C.: 1979a.

National Association for Foreign Student Affairs. *Standards and Responsibilities in International Educational Exchange*. Washington, D.C.: Winter 1979b.

National Association of State Universities and Land-Grant Colleges. *Project Proposal to National Science Foundation for Preparation of Material for the U.S. Delegation to the 1979 U.N. Conference on Science and Technology for Development*. Washington, D.C.: Jan. 1978a.

National Association of State Universities and Land-Grant Colleges. *Draft Code of Practice for Universities Involved in International Activities.* Washington, D.C.: 1978b.

National Endowment for the Humanities. *The National Endowment for the Humanities and International Education.* Washington, D.C.: Aug. 1978.

Nehrt, L. (Ed.). *Business and International Education.* Report submitted to the Government/Academic Interface Committee, International Education Project. Occasional Paper 4. Washington, D.C.: American Council on Education, May 1977.

Nisbet, R. "The Idea of Progress." Unpublished manuscript, American Academy of Arts and Sciences, 1977.

Nunn, C. Z., Crockett, H. J., Jr., and Williams, J. A., Jr. *Tolerance for Nonconformity: A National Survey of America's Changing Commitment to Civil Liberties.* San Francisco: Jossey-Bass, 1978.

O'Leary, J. "Five-Year Plan to Emphasize Third World Issues." *Times Higher Education Supplement* (London), Aug. 4, 1978.

Perkins, J. A. *International Programs of U.S. Colleges and Universities.* New York: International Council for Educational Development, 1971.

Perkins, J. A. In "Worldwide Worry Over New Restrictions on Academic Mobility." *Times Educational Supplement* (London), Oct. 1, 1978, p. 6.

Pike, L., and Barrows, T. S. "Other Nations, Other Peoples: A Survey of Student Interests, Knowledge, Attitudes, and Perceptions." Unpublished manuscript, Washington, D.C., U.S. Department of Health, Education, and Welfare, 1976.

Reischauer, E. O. *Toward the Twenty-First Century.* New York: Random House, 1973.

Reston, J. B. "The Press and International Understanding." In R. J. Armbruster (Ed.), *A Process of Global Enlightenment.* Washington, D.C.: Board of Foreign Scholarships, Nov. 1976.

Rielly, J. E. (Ed.). *American Public Opinion and U.S. Foreign Policy.* Chicago: Chicago Council on Foreign Relations, 1979.

Rosenau, J. N. *International Studies in the University: Some Problems and Issues for the 1970s.* Paper prepared for International Council for Educational Development Conference on the Potential of U.S. International Studies in the 1970s, April 1-3, 1971. (Mimeo.)

Rosenau, J. N. *The Attentive Public in an Interdependent World: A Survey of Theoretical Perspectives and Empirical Findings.* Report prepared for the Columbus Transnational Project, sponsored by the Mershon Center for Programs of Research and Education in Leadership in Public Policy. Columbus: Ohio State University Press, Oct. 1972.

Rosenthal, E. L. "Lifelong Learning—For Some of the People." *Change,* Aug. 1977, *9* (8).

Sanders, I. T., and Ward, J. C. *Bridges to Understanding.* Carnegie Commission on Higher Education. New York: McGraw-Hill, 1970.

Santinelli, P. "Decision Makers Need More International Cooperation." *Times Higher Education Supplement* (London), Oct. 20, 1978, p. 3.

"Scandinavian Hornet's Nest." *Times Higher Education Supplement* (London), April 29, 1977.

Schneider, A. I. "NDEA Centers: How They Use Their Federal Money." Paper prepared for the President's Commission, Office of Education, U.S. Department of Health, Education, and Welfare, Dec. 26, 1978.

Scully, M. G. "Decline in Foreign-Language Study May Be Ending." *Chronicle of Higher Education*, May 30, 1978, *16* (14).

Shannon, W. G. *A Survey of International/Intercultural Education in Two-Year Colleges.* La Plata, Md.: Charles County Community College, Nov. 1978.

Smith, T. "Gains of the President's Trip." *New York Times*, April 4, 1978.

Solomon, L. D. *Multinational Corporations and the Emerging World Order.* New York: Kennikat Press, 1978.

Starr, S. F. "English Dethroned." *Change*, May 1978a, *10* (5).

Starr, S. F. Statement at the meeting of the President's Commission on Foreign Language and International Studies, Washington, D.C., Oct. 27, 1978b.

Sterling, C. H., and Haight, T. R. *The Mass Media: Aspen Institute Guide to Communication Industry Trends.* New York: Praeger, 1978.

Sullivan, G. (Rapporteur). *U.S. Research on the U.S.S.R. and Eastern Europe: A Critical Resource for Security and Commercial Policy.* Washington, D.C.: Center for Strategic and International Studies, Georgetown University, 1977.

Swayzee, C. O. *International Training and Research in the Ford Foundation 1951-1966: A Draft Report.* New York: Ford Foundation, June 1967.

"Ten Years of Foreign Affairs Research." *FAR Horizons*, Winter 1977, *10* (1).

Thistlethwaite, F. *The Mobility of Students and Staff Internationally.* Twelfth Commonwealth Universities Congress. Vancouver: Association of Commonwealth Universities, Aug. 19-25, 1978.

"Tight Market for College Teachers." *Ford Foundation Letter*, Feb. 1, 1977, *8* (1).

"Too Many Pupils Put Off Languages." *Times Educational Supplement* (London), May 26, 1978.

Touraine, A. *The Academic System in American Society.* Carnegie Commission on Higher Education. New York: McGraw-Hill, 1974.

United Nations Educational, Scientific, and Cultural Organization. *Foreign Student Statistics, 1969-1973.* No. 21. Paris: 1975.

"U.N. Sees Population Rise Slowing." *New York Times*, June 28, 1978.

U.S. Arms Control and Disarmament Agency. *Report to Congress on Arms Control Education and Academic Study Centers.* Washington, D.C.: Jan. 1979. (Mimeo.)

U.S. Bureau of the Census. *Statistical Abstracts of the United States.* Washington, D.C.: U.S. Government Printing Office, 1974.

U.S. Bureau of Labor Statistics. *Occupational Outlook for College Graduates.* Washington, D.C.: U.S. Government Printing Office, 1978.

U.S. Department of Commerce, Travel Service. *Summary Analysis of In-*

ternational Travel To/From the U.S., 1976 and Historical Series from 1960; Statistics on International Travel by Residents of Foreign Countries. Washington, D.C.: n.d.

U.S. Department of Health, Education, and Welfare, Office of Education. "Modern Foreign-Language and Area Studies." In *Federal Register*, May 23, 1977, *42* (99), chap. 1.

U.S. Department of Health, Education, and Welfare, Office of Education. "Part 146a—Citizen Education for Cultural Understanding Program." In *Federal Register*, May 12, 1978a, *43* (93).

U.S. Department of Health, Education, and Welfare, Office of Education, Division of International Education, International Studies Branch. *NDEA International Studies Programs at the Undergraduate Level, Distribution of Federal Support, 1972-1978*. Washington, D.C.: 1978b. (Mimeo.)

U.S. General Accounting Office. *Summary of Views and Observations Expressed at the GAO Symposium Held on International Exchange-of-Persons Programs*. Washington, D.C.: Dec. 14, 1976. (Mimeo.)

U.S. General Accounting Office, Comptroller General. *Greater U.S. Government Efforts Needed to Recruit Qualified Candidates for Employment by U.N. Organizations*. Washington, D.C.: U.S. Government Printing Office, May 16, 1977a.

U.S. General Accounting Office. *International Education and Cultural Exchange-of-Persons Programs, Approved Work Plans, International Division*. Washington, D.C.: May 26, 1977b.

U.S. General Accounting Office, Comptroller General. *Coordination of International Exchange and Training Programs: Opportunities and Limitations*. Washington, D.C.: July 24, 1978a.

U.S. General Accounting Office, Comptroller General. *Report to the Congress of the United States. Study of Foreign Languages and Related Areas: Federal Support, Administration, Need*. Washington, D.C.: 1978b.

Vance, C. R. "Meeting the Challenges of a Changing World." Speech before the American Association of Community and Junior Colleges. Chicago, May 1, 1979. (Department of State Press Release no. 116, May 1, 1979.)

Walker, D. "Report Points to Gaps in Area Studies Coverage." *Times Higher Education Supplement* (London), July 29, 1977.

Ward, R. E. *National Needs for International Education*. Washington, D.C.: Center for Strategic and International Studies, Georgetown University, 1977.

Wiegner, K. "Can't Somebody Turn the Damned Thing Off?" *Forbes*, Aug. 7, 1978.

Winks, R. W. "A Report on Some Aspects of the Fulbright-Hays Program." Unpublished paper prepared for Council on International Change of Scholars. Washington, D.C., Feb. 15, 1977.

World Bank. *World Development Report 1978*. Washington, D.C.: Aug. 1978.

"Worldwide Worry over New Restrictions on Academic Mobility." *Times Higher Education Supplement* (London), Oct. 1, 1978.

Yankelovich, D. *The New Morality: A Profile of American Youth in the '70s.* New York: McGraw-Hill, 1974.

Yankelovich, D. *Jobs and Work.* Presentation to a preliminary meeting at the Aspen Institute on Financing the Future. New York: Aspen Institute for Humanistic Studies, May 1, 1978.

Index